Lincoln's Decision for Emancipation

Hans L. Trefousse

Brooklyn College / City University of New York

The America's Alternatives Series

Edited by **Harold M. Hyman**

Lincoln's Decision for Emancipation

J.B. Lippincott Company
Philadelphia / New York / Toronto

ISBN 0-397-47336-2
Library of Congress Catalog Card Number 74-28125
Printed in the United States of America\

1 3 5 7 9 8 6 4 2

Library of Congress Cataloging in Publication Data

Trefousse, Hans Louis.
    Lincoln's decision for emancipation.

    (The America's alternatives series)
    Bibliography: p.
    1. United States—Politics and government—Civil
War, 1861-1865. 2. Lincoln, Abraham, Pres. U.S.,
1809-1865—Views on slavery. 3. Slavery in the United
States—Emancipation. 4. Emancipation proclamation.
I. Title.
E453.T79   320.9'73'07   74-28125
ISBN 0-397-47336-2

TO THE MEMORY OF
LISL BRESLAUER

Contents

Foreword

"When you judge decisions, you have to judge them in the light of what there was available to do it," noted Secretary of State George C. Marshall to the Senate Committees on the Armed Services and Foreign Relations in May 1951.[1] In this spirit, each volume in the "America's Alternatives" series examines the past for insights which History—perhaps only History—is peculiarly fitted to offer. In each volume the author seeks to learn why decision makers in crucial public policy or, more rarely, private choice situations adopted a course and rejected others. Within this context of choices, the author may ask what influence then-existing expert opinion, administrative structures, and budgetary factors exerted in shaping decisions? What weights did constitutions or traditions have? What did men hope for or fear? On what information did they base their decisions? Once a decision was made, how was the decision maker able to enforce it? What attitudes prevailed toward nationality, race, region, religion, or sex, and how did these attitudes modify results?

We freely ask such questions of the events of our time. This "America's Alternatives" volume transfers appropriate versions of such queries to the past.

In examining those elements that were a part of a crucial historical decision, the author has refrained from making judgments based upon attitudes, information, or values that were not current at the time the decision was made. Instead, as much as possible he or she has explored the past in terms of data and prejudices known to persons contemporary to the event.

1. U.S., Senate, Hearings Before the Committees on the Armed Services and the Foreign Relations of the United States, *The Military Situation in the Far East*, 82d Cong., 2d sess., part I, p. 382. Professor Ernest R. May's "Alternatives" volume directed me to this source and quotation.

Nevertheless, the following reconstruction of one of America's major alternative choices speaks implicitly and frequently, explicitly to present concerns.

In form, this volume consists of a narrative and analytical historical essay (Part One), within which the author has identified by use of headnotes (i.e., *Alternative 1*, etc.) the choices which he believes were actually before the decision makers with whom he is concerned.

Part Two of this volume contains, in whole or part, the most appropriate source documents that illustrate the Part One Alternatives. The Part Two Documents and Part One essay are keyed for convenient use (i.e., references in Part One will direct readers to appropriate Part Two Documents). The volume's Part Three offers users further guidance in the form of a Bibliographic Essay.

In the century since 1865, Lincoln was considered to be the president most worthy of biracial respect. In substantial part he held this lofty place because of his decision in favor of ending slavery. Recently, his reputation as emancipating hero has suffered a sharp reversal. Lincoln has even been maligned by some commentators as a racist, opportunistic "honkey."

The ethics, values, and credibility of America's political leaders is an important matter, a century ago as now. Professor Hans L. Trefousse, one of the most important commentators on the men and measures of the Civil War and Reconstruction, offers in this volume a review of Lincoln's options centering on slavery that will advance the ongoing debate about that president's qualities.

Harold M. Hyman
Rice University

Preface

Of all the decisions Abraham Lincoln made, his determination to emancipate the slaves was probably the most far-reaching. Why he made it, how he made it, and what he might or might not have done, has ever since been a fertile field for contention. Was Lincoln a convinced opponent of slavery? Was he interested in uplifting the submerged race? Or was he nothing but a cynical pragmatist who cared nothing for black suffering? Was he an idealistic benefactor of mankind, or was he interested only in furthering military and political objectives for the well-being of the whites? The answers to these questions provide the key not only to Lincoln's character, but in a larger sense, to the fundamental issues of the Civil War as well.

In 1861, when war broke out, it was by no means certain that the new president would attack slavery. He had gone on record again and again against interference with the domestic institutions of the states, and had refused to denounce the Fugitive Slave Law. Northern abolitionists had called him the "slave hound from Illinois." It is true that he had adamantly refused to consider any compromise on the issue of nonextension of slavery, the question upon which he had been elected, but he had also endorsed the pending constitutional amendment which would have spelled out in more detail the inability of Congress to interfere with the institution in those states in which it already existed. Farsighted observers might predict that the war would surely bring with it the destruction of the Southern social systems; if the president thought such developments likely, he prudently kept his opinions to himself.

That Lincoln was personally opposed to slavery is really not open to dispute. As early as 1837, when he was a member of the Illinois Assembly, he denounced the institution. When in 1847 he went to Congress, he joined Joshua R. Giddings, the most outspoken antislavery leader in the House, in cosponsoring a measure for the abolition of involuntary servitude in the District of Columbia. In 1854, denouncing the repeal of the Missouri Compromise, he again emphasized his dislike of bondage. In part it was his outspoken condemnation of slavery which, in 1858, brought him the Republican senatorial endorsement. Then, in his famous debates with Stephen A. Douglas, whether or not he conceded the alleged racial inferiority of the Negro, he not only reaffirmed his conviction that blacks were entitled to the fruit of their own labor but went so far as to reiterate what he had said earlier. Slavery must eventually disappear. His credentials as an opponent of the Southern social system were impeccable.

But no matter how much the president abhorred the "peculiar institution," he had an excellent sense of timing. A supreme pragmatist, he rarely sought the unattainable. Given the precarious position of the United States in 1861, he could hardly be expected to fly in the face of popular opinion and preach an abolitionist crusade. Especially not when four slave states and portions of others remained loyal and had to be humored.

With these conditions in mind, Lincoln carefully sought to reassure his listeners. Quoting from one of his former speeches that it was not his purpose, directly or indirectly, to interfere with the institution of slavery in the states where it existed, he specifically reiterated these sentiments in his first inaugural address. He repeatedly stated that the war was not being fought for the purpose of eradicating slavery. It was being waged solely for the purpose of restoring the Union.

This book, as well as the series, *America's Alternatives*, owes its inspiration to Dr. Harold M. Hyman, William P. Hobby Professor of History at Rice University. He established the format and supplied valuable editorial advice, and I should like to express my appreciation to him.

But of course in the long run the war did become a crusade against slavery, as well as a struggle for the restoration of the federal Union. Why Lincoln deliberately chose this road and what alternatives he had constitutes the subject of this essay.

Hans L. Trefousse
Brooklyn College
City University of New York

Part One

Lincoln's Decision for Emancipation

1

The Problem and Its Possible Solutions

When in April 1861 Abraham Lincoln was confronted with the harsh reality of civil war, the problems he faced seemed nearly insurmountable. It is true that in population, the loyal states outnumbered those seceding by more than two to one, and twice that number if only whites are counted. It is also true that the North possessed an infinitely larger industrial plant, had a much greater per capita income, and disposed of much more capital and of incomparably more resources than the South. But in order to win, in order to break up the attempt to found a rival nation, it had to conquer the disaffected section completely. The insurgents' military forces must be destroyed, their territory seized, their will to fight broken. Would Northern public opinion unflinchingly sustain the president in a war that might last a long time and become very costly?

There were many who thought the answer was no. After all, Abraham Lincoln was a minority president. More votes had been cast against him than for him, and in many loyal states, there were powerful Democratic organizations which had long cooperated with Southern colleagues. Commercial bonds tied the eastern seaboard to the cotton states. The Mississippi River and its tributaries constituted the great connecting artery of the Midwest. Could the northwestern states along the river banks be persuaded that they ought to fight to the last against those who had so long been their trading partners? Or would they not prefer to make some compromise arrangement, an agreement which would permit them to resume their accustomed commercial patterns without too much difficulty?

The attitude of the border states was even more dubious. Although Kentucky, Missouri, Maryland, and Delaware had not seceded, and the western part of Virginia had refused to go along with the rest of the state, public opinion in all of these slaveholding commonwealths was divided. Their interests bound them to the South as well as to the North, and the slightest misstep of the federal government might precipitate one or several of them into secession. And so important was their strategic value that Lincoln himself believed their continued adherence to the Union essential.

The chief difficulty in maintaining the loyalty of the Democrats, and especially of the border states, was the slavery question. Somehow people everywhere sensed that the "peculiar institution" was the principal cause of

3

the war, and if they had any doubts, Alexander H. Stephens in his notorious Cornerstone Address disabused them. "The new Constitution," the Confederate vice-president said at Savannah on March 21, 1861, "has put to rest forever all the agitating questions relating to our peculiar institution—African slavery as it exists among us—the proper status of the negro in our form of civilization. This was the immediate cause of the late rupture and present revolution." Then he proceeded to explain that the cornerstone of the new government rested on the "truth" that the Negro was not the equal of the white man and that slavery, "subordination to the superior race," was his natural and moral condition.[1] While many Democrats were willing to fight to preserve the Union, they were not willing to take issue with the defenders of slavery.

The importance of the slavery problem to the border states was evident from the very beginning. As long as the institution existed there, Southern hopes for their eventual adherence would never fade. To do away with bondage, however, would alienate important Unionist factions. And the president was determined not to do anything that would jeopardize Unionism in the loyal slave states.

The moment hostilities began, it was clear that the government might have to deal with slavery in some way. But the question was, how? To be sure, the vocal though numerically weak radical element in the North had always advocated a policy of immediate emancipation; neither the administration nor the majority of the population, however, was willing to go along with the proposition. The border states were naturally opposed to any interference with their domestic institutions, and the Northern Democrats, by no means a small group, largely agreed with them (see Documents 4, 7, and 8). Even some conservative Republicans were appalled at the thought of abolishing slavery at once (see Document 3).

Northern and Southern Racial Prejudices: Obstacles to Emancipation

One of the chief problems in dealing with the Southern labor system was the widespread racial prejudice which existed in the United States, not only in the South, but also in the North. Slavery was generally confined to Negroes, and Negroes, if they were held to be human at all, were almost everywhere considered an inferior race. In nineteenth-century America, Chief Justice Roger B. Taney's assertion that they were regarded as beings of an inferior order, with no rights the white man was bound to respect, was not far from the truth. Pamphlets and books explained the inability of the black race ever to establish self-government (see Document 1). Africa was thought to be a truly dark continent, bereft of civilization, given over to barbarism, and inhabited by cannibals. Thus it was thought to provide proof of the blacks' inferiority. That the Negro Republic of Haiti had not flourished was also cited as an example of the blacks' alleged incapacity to manage their own affairs. Most Americans did not believe that the Negro ought to be enslaved, but neither did they believe that he ought to be given equal rights.

Because of this widespread prejudice, the franchise was restricted to whites in most Northern states. Where this was not the case, either there were very few Negroes or those entitled to vote had to pay taxes not required of whites. Generally kept from the public schools, denied elementary civil and political rights, and confined in noisome ghettos, the Northern blacks eked out a miserable existence. That their poverty did not contribute to a lessening of the unfavorable attitudes towards them is not surprising. Some states attempted to exclude them altogether, and Republican speakers often stressed their conviction that the western territories were regions destined for white settlers and white settlers only.

Not even leading Republicans were exempt from the general feeling of prejudice against color. In 1850, Salmon P. Chase, one of the few public figures who was generally free from the all-pervasive racism of the time, felt compelled to caution C.H. and J.M. Langston, the two black leaders who had solicited his opinion on colonization. "The state of public sentiment is such. . . ," he replied, "as to preclude the idea that the people of color in Ohio can expect equality of rights with the whites at present."[2] Ten years later, the radical Illinois Congressman Owen Lovejoy, whose brother Elijah was the first martyr of the abolitionist cause, stated in the House: "We may concede it as a matter of fact that it [the black race] is inferior."[3] During the war, the later senator from Wisconsin, Timothy O. Howe, wrote to William Pitt Fessenden: "I regard the freedmen, in the main . . . as so much animal life—educated to labor but unused to direct its efforts or to appreciate its results."[4] C.H. Ray, the Chicago journalist who in 1860 had played a significant role in the nomination of Lincoln, was probably correct when, in 1866, he wrote to his friend Lyman Trumbull: "The prejudice against the Negro is not wholly overborne. Say what we may, you and I share it; and what is true of us is doubly true of others. . . . The masses give way to prejudice uncontrolled; and to dislike, I will not say to hate a negro is just as natural as to distinguish black from white."[5] If these were the opinions of leading Republicans, the Democrats' racism soon became the chief talking point in their quest for political preferment. As Lincoln, speaking of the general aversion to granting blacks social and political equality, pointed out as early as 1854, "Whether this feeling accords with justice and sound judgment is not the sole question, if indeed it is any part of it. A universal feeling, whether well or ill founded cannot be safely disregarded."[6]

What made this prejudice even more dangerous was the very real fear of economic competition. What was to prevent freed slaves from coming north and competing with white laborers? Although the argument lacked substance, it was widely accepted. Workers of all types, and especially recent Irish immigrants, not only looked down upon the Negro; they feared him as well. The Democrats never failed to play upon their apprehensions.

If white Americans did not care for blacks, they also believed that the federal government had no right to set Negroes free. Constitutional restraints were considered binding, and the basic charter delegated no powers either to Congress or to the president to interfere with the domestic institutions of the states, which included definitions of property law defining and nurturing slavery. Not even the outbreak of war changed this fact, and Lincoln was as aware of it as anybody. It was for the purpose of preserving the Constitution that he had called on citizens to come to the aid of the government and possibly lay down their lives; that same Constitution provided no sanctions for interference with the "peculiar institution" within the states where it was legal.

Factors Favorable to Change: Lincoln's Alternatives

Nevertheless, changes might come. Slavery was, after all, basic to the Southern way of life, and the South was engaged in a rebellion against the government. Was it not to be expected that its cherished institution, like everything else, sooner or later might be affected by military operations? Was it not likely that in time, Northern strategists would come to the conclusion that it was in their interest to deprive the insurgents of the support of an undraftable laboring class, an element which would at the same time favor the Union? Would not sheer military necessity oblige federal commanders to replenish their armies with black men?

In addition, it was likely that the mere presence of hostile armies in a slave area would loosen the bondsmen's restraints. The reappearance of the federal flag in a war against slaveholders would undoubtedly induce any number of blacks to seek freedom under its shelter. In the long run, Northern officers and soldiers could not be expected to return them to their insurgent owners.

Other factors could be counted upon to undermine slavery as well. Many of the South's calculations were predicated on the hope of European recognition and aid. Two years before the war, Senator James H. Hammond of South Carolina declared that cotton was king and that no power on earth dared wage war upon it. The entire world was allegedly dependent upon Southern cotton, the argument ran; if cotton were withheld for three years, England would topple headlong and carry the civilized world with her. Consequently, Great Britain and possibly France would sooner or later have to interfere to secure their uninterrupted supply of cotton. And their interference would mean recognition and independence of the South.

But there was another side to this argument. American abolitionists were not working in isolation. The antislavery movement was worldwide and generally popular in Europe. During the course of the nineteenth century, slavery had been abolished in most developed countries. By 1861, in the New World, other than the Southern states, only Brazil and the Spanish colonies of Cuba and Puerto Rico still tolerated human bondage. Britain and France especially had strongly supported the antislavery crusade. No matter how hostile Lord Palmerston's cabinet might be to the United States, it was still opposed to chattel slavery. Emancipation would make it very difficult for any European power to recognize the Confederacy or to interfere in its favor in the Civil War.

Considering these factors, Lincoln had several alternative courses of action at his disposal. He could leave the problem to Congress, which might or might not take action on its own. If he himself was to initiate policy—his usual course—he could adhere to the radical program of freeing all the slaves and turn the conflict into a war for freedom. He could also reject the radicals' advice and free none of the slaves, thus maintaining his position that the object of the war was the preservation of the Union, and not the abolition of slavery. Finally, he could free some of the slaves and keep others in bondage, at least temporarily. Should he decide to free some or all of the slaves, he would have the option of doing so either by proclamation or by local action, which would permit military commanders to erode the institution. He could adopt the policy of emancipation either immediately or gradually, with or without compensation. Finally, he had to make up his mind what to do with the freedmen, should emancipation become a reality. They might be drafted into the army, they might be used as laborers or they might be colonized abroad, either with or without their consent. All these alternatives were considered at one time or another.

The advantages of not freeing any slaves were fairly obvious (*Alternative 1:* see Documents 3, 4, 7, and 8). The all-important border states would be strengthened in their loyalty; Northern Democrats would be deprived of an issue, and no cries of incitement to race warfare could be raised against the administration. On the other hand, however, such a policy would permit the South to reap the benefits of slavery in wartime. Southern bondsmen would be compelled to work for their insurgent masters; Southern whites would be freed from nonmilitary labor to serve in the army, and a potential allied force of almost four million loyal people would be allowed to be totally disregarded. In addition, practical considerations of what to do with individual fugitives would demand solution. It was impossible to wage war in a slaveholding area without becoming entangled in the institution, and the army would demand some sort of instructions on how to deal with the prickly problem.

A general policy of emancipation, on the other hand, also had evident advantages (*Alternative 2:* see Document 11). In the first place, it would satisfy the increasingly militant wing of Lincoln's own party. By inspiring idealistic Northerners with a new and noble cause, the administration might counteract temporary setbacks on the battlefield. It would also solve the difficult problem of the disposition of runaway slaves, and create a firmly loyal force in the South. Above all, it would make it almost impossible for foreign countries to recognize the Confederacy. Emancipation would be a diplomatic trump card. And finally, given the president's own long-matured antislavery views, it could not be distasteful for him to become the emancipator of an entire race.

But the disadvantages of a general emancipation policy had to give the administration pause. What effect would such action have on the wavering border states? Would it not precipitate them into headlong secession? Would not the announcement of what was considered an abolitionist measure totally alienate many Northern Democrats, heretofore loyal to the government? At the very least, it would create tremendous difficulties for border state Unionists and present a new issue to Democrats everywhere; at most it might cause the loss of some or all of the border states and near rebellion in the North. In addition, there was the problem of the army. Would officers and men of conservative background, willing to fight for the Union and Constitution, be equally willing to remain active if the war were to become a struggle against slavery? And how would the sudden emancipation of the blacks be received by a population which, though not particularly fond of slavery, nevertheless harbored deep prejudices against the potential freedmen?

There was, finally, the possibility of freeing some of the blacks and leaving others in slavery (*Alternative 3:* see Documents 9, 10, and 15). This course of action might avoid some of the disadvantages of the other two alternatives, while securing the advantages of both. Of course, it had its own drawbacks. Piecemeal measures might not be considered enough of a commitment by the radicals and might be deemed too radical to suit the conservatives. Timing and the exact wording of any document to be promulgated were of the essence.

In case the government decided to emancipate some or all of the Negroes, the various alternatives of conferring freedom upon them also had to be considered. On the one hand, it was possible to allow army commanders to free individual slaves in the course of military operations. In pursuing this course, the administration would have to take no overt steps to renounce its commitment to a war for the maintenance of the Union alone. The border states would not be directly affected, and Northern Democrats might acquiesce in military liberation more easily than in any other. On the other hand, such a procedure would largely negate the favorable effects of emancipation abroad; nor would it satisfy abolitionists and radicals. A specific Emancipation Proclamation, on the contrary, would secure all these advantages.

The question of compensation likewise created problems (*Alternative 4:* see Document 6). Any large-scale policy of paying for slaves would be costly. It would require the concurrence of Congress, which might be difficult to obtain. Conversely, it would avoid the ticklish question of confiscation of private property, and would lessen conservative opposition.

The timing of emancipation, if decided upon, also had to be carefully considered. Gradual steps might lessen the impact upon the border states and the Democrats, but they would disappoint radicals and make no impression on foreign emancipationists. But while a sudden decision would not encounter these drawbacks, it would have to be made at a time when political, military, and diplomatic conditions were exactly right.

Alternative Procedures After Emancipation

What to do with the freedmen themselves was another question susceptible to several answers. There were those who argued for their inclusion in the army as full-fledged soldiers (*Alternative 5:* see Document 15). Why should the blacks not be asked to fight for their own liberty? And why should a nation, hard pressed for manpower, overlook so large a pool of willing recruits? This problem too could be solved in a piecemeal fashion, or it could be solved all at once. Negroes might at first be drafted as laborers and service personnel, and only with time be promoted to more active service. The transition to a policy of military employment of ex-slaves would then be easier. It was to be expected that any utilization of black soldiers would bring forth anguished protests from border state politicians fearful for the safety of the "peculiar institution;" it was also certain that it would be attacked by the more active Negro haters in the North. Many confirmed racists had long been arguing that blacks were incapable of standing up to an organized enemy, although others attempted to refute them by citing obvious historical examples to the contrary. And there might be charges of attempting to instigate a race war, accusations which could have very serious repercussions abroad. Again, the timing and wording of any measure designed to facilitate Negro military service would be of the utmost importance.

Finally, there was the question of colonization (*Alternative 6:* see Document 13). In view of the existing prejudice against blacks, the idea of sending freedmen back to Africa or of establishing colonies for them in the Caribbean and elsewhere had long been popular. The American Colonization Society, which had existed since the beginning of the century, had succeeded in establishing the Republic of Liberia. It was clear to most rational observers that the magnitude of the undertaking rendered a total resettlement of more than a fraction of American blacks chimerical, but the idea continued to have general appeal. Lincoln himself had long favored colonization, but his innate good sense and moral stamina inclined him against any forced policy of emigration. Thus for all practical purposes the only policy he seriously considered was that of voluntary emigration. The extent and direction of this movement, however, long remained a fruitful field for discussion.

Advocates of colonization tended to stress the alleged impossibility of the two races living in the same community as social and political equals. Given these facts, they argued, both Negroes and whites would be better off if they separated. Of course the sheer weight of numbers seemed to militate against the undertaking; in addition, some radicals argued that the Negroes, enslaved through no fault of their own, had a perfect right to remain in the land of their birth. It was also said that black laborers were urgently needed in America, and that colonization would deprive the country of a valuable laboring force. Nevertheless, widespread fears in the North that freedmen would flock across Mason's and Dixon's line to compete with white workers made talk of colonization an attractive political ploy.

Lincoln's Sources of Information and Advice

Although the president had the responsibility for the ultimate decisions about emancipation, he did not arrive at his conclusions in a vacuum. Bureaucratic habits, constitutional patterns, fiscal problems, public attitudes, and popular prejudices all had to be taken into consideration. These factors strongly influenced Lincoln's choices. Nevertheless, he was always careful to insist upon and exercise his final authority. This was especially true in dealing with slavery.

The sources of information available to the president were varied. In the first place, the War Department telegraph kept him minutely informed about military and related developments. A frequent visitor to the Military Telegraph Office, Lincoln established a close working relationship with Major Thomas D. Eckart, the supervisor of military telegraphs.

The newspapers were another source of information. To be sure, most of the journals sent to the White House never reached Lincoln, but his private secretaries saw to it that the three Washington dailies—the *Morning Chronicle*, the *National Republican*, and the *Evening Star* were available to him on a table in his study. In addition, they clipped interesting items from the Southern press and presented them to him. How much time he was able to devote to newspapers is uncertain, although he was inordinately fond of such humorous writers as Artemus Ward (Charles F. Brown) and Petroleum V. Nasby (David Ross Locke). According to Noah Brooks, the president did find leisure to read the papers, or, as he sometimes expressed it, " 'to skirmish' with them."[7] Since the press, both friendly and hostile, was filled with articles touching on slavery, he was kept well informed about changing currents of thought.

Private correspondents also permitted the president to feel the pulse of the nation. How many of his letters he read in person is difficult to tell, but it is clear that he paid attention to a good number of them. At least his annotations and endorsements would seem to bear out his interest in private sources of information. Among his correspondents were such well known public figures as the historian George Bancroft, who often communicated with Lincoln on the subject of slavery, the French Protestant leader Agénor de Gasparin, Giuseppe Garibaldi, and other foreign and domestic leaders of public opinion. Various editors of newspapers—Joseph Medill of the Chicago *Tribune*, Henry J. Raymond of the *New York Times*, and Horace Greeley of the New York *Tribune*, for example—were also frequent correspondents. And old friends and acquaintances back in Illinois often wrote simple letters of advice to their distinguished former neighbor.

In addition to letters addressed to himself, the president also saw copies of communications to powerful politicians. Charles Sumner, for example, anxious to convert Lincoln to his brand of radicalism, sent him excerpts of letters received, while Francis P. Blair, Sr., equally desirous of keeping the president conservative, used the same tactics. Lincoln seemed to be receptive to all these influences.

Another way of keeping in touch with popular trends was the custom of receiving delegations of concerned citizens, who were frequently welcomed at the White House. Representing numerous factions, the delegations pressed their different points of view upon their host. Again and again spokesmen for various religious denominations visited the chief executive to inform him of the certain will of God. Usually they favored immediate emancipation, but deputations of loyal citizens from the border states also arrived to plead for the exact opposite. Anxious to keep in touch with the people, Lincoln was rarely too busy to give a respectful hearing to the many visitors who came to see him.

Of course the president was not confined to information furnished by obvious public sources. He received lengthy reports from all his military commanders, and such officers as General Benjamin F. Butler, first at Fort Monroe and later at New Orleans, Generals David Hunter and Rufus P. Saxton in the Department of the South, and George B. McClellan in Virginia furnished especially pertinent information about the "peculiar institution." The solicitor of the War Department, William Whiting, wrote lengthy explanations of the constitutional implications of emancipation (see Document 2), and after the winter of 1862, additional facts could be obtained from Edward L. Pierce, who was conducting an experiment with black labor in the Sea Islands under the auspices of the Treasury Department. The confidential reports of American ministers abroad also frequently dealt with the problem of slavery.

One of the most important sources of information available to Lincoln was his personal contact with members of Congress and other political leaders. Frequently pictured as having been at odds with the radical faction of his own party (see Document 16), in reality, the president knew very well how to cooperate with party leaders at the other side of Pennsylvania Avenue (see Document 17). Sumner in particular became friendly with both the president and Mrs. Lincoln. As chairman of the Senate Committee on Foreign Relations, he not only loyally cooperated with the administration in solving pressing diplomatic problems, but he often visited the Lincolns to discourse on other matters. Emancipation was his principal interest.

Other radical members of Congress also had access to the White House. Personal relations between the president and Benjamin F. Wade of Ohio and Zachariah Chandler of Michigan were often strained, but this state of affairs did not prevent the two radicals from voicing their opinions freely and seeing the chief executive frequently. The members of the Joint Committee on the Conduct of the War, chaired by Wade, often obtained interviews. As spokesmen for the radicals in general, they could be relied upon to press for more vigorous policies in dealing with slavery as well as in the prosecution of the war. Their zeal was a good indicator of radical opinion.

More moderate and conservative legislators also met with the president. Representatives from the border states often conferred with him, and travelers from occupied areas also visited the White House. In addition, he was on close personal terms with the conservative Republican senator from Illinois, Orville H. Browning, who often came to call and discuss public affairs.

And then there was the cabinet. Purposely chosen to reflect a variety of opinions, the secretaries rarely agreed completely on any issue. Secretary of the Treasury Salmon P. Chase, and to some extent Secretary of War Simon

Cameron, often urged radical measures; Attorney General Edward Bates, Secretary of the Navy Gideon Welles, and Secretary of State William H. Seward advised caution. When Edwin M. Stanton displaced Cameron at the War Department, he generally favored the radicals, while Postmaster General Montgomery Blair, after a brief period of radical opposition to conciliation, became increasingly conservative. Caleb B. Smith, and his successor John P. Usher, in the Department of the Interior were not as influential as their colleagues, but since the department contained an office for emigration and Smith was an advocate of colonization, Lincoln consulted with him on the subject. While the president did not rely on the secretaries as a "team," he was nevertheless attentive to their individual opinions, and they had easy access to him. The vice-president, Hannibal Hamlin, a radical from Maine, also enjoyed Lincoln's confidence. If we are to trust his grandson, Hamlin was the first person to learn about Lincoln's decision to issue an Emancipation Proclamation.

The governors of the loyal states were another channel of communication which the president valued. Frequently reporting on the status of public opinion and of affairs within their commonwealths, they enabled him to obtain significant information from every part of the Union. Since most of them belonged to his own political party, he had the advantage of confidential advice which is so essential for a chief executive.

Prominent persons outside regular government channels also freely offered their counsel. Carl Schurz, the influential German-American leader, was an honored guest at the White House as early as spring, 1861. He played the piano for his host and unabashedly tried to enlighten him on a multitude of subjects ranging from music to emancipation. Although he sometimes annoyed the president by his conceit and self-righteousness, the channels of communications between the two were never broken, and Schurz remained a firm advocate of antislavery principles. Thurlow Weed, the New York political manipulator known as the "Wizard of the Lobby," attempted to exert influence of a conservative nature both in person and through his friend Seward. Lincoln listened to him as to others, and despite the cares of office in the midst of war, never neglected his contacts with spokesmen for the most varied groups of partisans.

The Impact of Bureaucratic Habits

Existing bureaucratic habits greatly affected the president's decisions about slavery. The sudden conversion of the federal establishment from a languorous amorphous group of officials to an efficient engine of war brought about many changes, but the deeply ingrained bureaucratic channels were difficult if not impossible to alter. Law and custom prevented blacks from even carrying the mails, and the average office holder could not really be expected to see in the freedmen, or would-be freedmen, a source for any sort of support. Like other Americans, civil servants were biased against nonwhites and had no sympathy for abolitionists.

Three major departments were primarily concerned with the question of slavery, although others became marginally involved. The War Department was directly affected because of the immediate problems created by fugitives encountered during military operations. As it was the principal agency to implement any conceivable decision to emancipate, the attitudes of its officials would be of special importance. Since both Cameron and especially Stanton tended to favor steps leading toward emancipation, Lincoln had at his disposal a bureaucracy which would prove very useful in overcoming its underlings' natural sluggishness. This effectiveness was heightened because the solicitor of the War Department, William Whiting, was also in favor of energetic policies and wrote learned works about the war powers of the president (see Document 2). After April, 1862, the War Department was also charged with running the experiment of black cultivation of lands at Beaufort and the surrounding Sea Islands in South Carolina (the Port Royal Experiment), a task of no mean proportions which was watched with great interest by the proponents of rights for freedmen.

The other department directly affected by the slavery question was the Treasury. In part this was due to Secretary Chase's great interest in emancipation, and in part to the financial implications of slave ownership. If runaway owners failed to pay their taxes, what would become of their slaves? Abandoned property could be considered contraband of war, and after General Butler applied this term to human beings as well, Southern blacks were often treated as captured enemy property. The agents of the Treasury on the scene became a principal source of information, and the department never lost its interest in emancipation.

The involvement of the Department of the Interior was due to the appointment of James Mitchell, a longtime officer of the American Colonization Society, as commissioner of emigration within the department. Although Secretary Smith largely ignored him, Mitchell took a prominent part in efforts at colonization and played an important role in the attempt to establish a colony of freedmen in Chiriqui on the isthmus of Panama. It seems to have been taken for granted that the Interior Department ought to be in charge of such experiments. Because of alleged coal deposits in Panama, the Navy Department also became entangled in the affair, and the diplomatic implications of both colonization and emancipation brought the State Department into the picture as well. The attorney general's opinions were also of interest to an executive who was highly conscious of his constitutional obligations.

The constitutional problems connected with the slavery issue were very much on the president's mind. In view of the existing popular attitude, it was generally understood by Democrats as well as by Republicans that the Constitution precluded federal interference with "the peculiar institution" within the slave states. Lincoln certainly shared this understanding. Since he held that his main objective ought to be the preservation of the Constitution, he was not about to violate it, as he repeatedly pointed out. But he was also commander-in-chief of the army and navy, and in this capacity, he became more and more convinced that in times of actual armed rebellion, in order to meet military necessities, he might be permitted to commit acts which he could not ordinarily justify as chief executive. The Emancipation Proclamation was predicated upon this assumption. To make it permanent, however, Lincoln always insisted that a constitutional amendment would have to be passed.

Popular attitudes towards government activities in the nineteenth century also had to be taken into consideration. That the government had the right to wage war and conduct foreign relations was generally conceded; grudgingly, it was also granted the power to levy taxes, operate the post office, and undertake certain public improvements. But everything else was dubious, and the right of any government, state or federal, to intrude in people's private economic affairs was often denied. Moreover, because of the widespread popular prejudice against Negroes, anything the government might do about emancipation was bound to be controversial.

The solution of the slavery problem, then, was a difficult one. Only by exercising extreme care as well as expert leadership could it be solved at all. Abraham Lincoln was ready to provide both.

Notes

1. Edward McPherson, ed., *The Political History of the United States of America During the Great Rebellion, 1860-1865* (Washington, 1865), pp. 103-4.

2. Chase to C.H. and J.M. Langston, November 11, 1850, Salmon P. Chase Papers, series 2, Library of Congress, Washington, D.C.

3. New York *Herald,* April 16, 1860.

4. Howe to W.P. Fessenden, August 28, 1864, T.O. Howe Papers, Wisconsin Historical Society, Madison, Wisconsin.

5. Ray to Trumbull, February 7, 1866, Lyman Trumbull Papers, Library of Congress, Washington, D.C.

6. Roy P. Basler, ed., *The Collected Works of Abraham Lincoln* (New Brunswick, N.J.: Rutgers University Press, 1953), vol. IV, p. 256.

7. Noah Brooks, *Washington in Lincoln's Time,* ed. Herbert Mitgang (New York: Rinehart & Co., 1958), p. 261.

2

Watchful Waiting

During the presidential campaign and the secession crisis of 1860-61, the slavery question was central. As the nominee of a party opposed to the spread of the "peculiar institution," Lincoln's fate depended upon it. He had to appeal simultaneously to conservatives frightened by abolitionism and to radicals anxious to strike a blow at slavery. In addition, he faced the dilemma which would plague him throughout his presidency: how to reconcile the two antagonistic wings of his own party. Differences in attitude towards slavery were the principal subjects of dispute between them. If he wanted to retain the support of both, he would have to handle the question with extreme care.

Because of his prudent course in the past, Lincoln was admirably suited to deal with this problem. Such veteran foes of slavery as Wade and Giddings were satisfied with his nomination, and although hostile newspapers called him an abolitionist, conservative Republicans were not unduly disturbed. Edward Bates, the conservative Missouri Whig who was to become his attorney general, knew that the nominee was committed to antislavery. But he considered him personally unobjectionable. Years later, Richard W. Thompson, Rutherford B. Hayes's conservative secretary of the navy, maintained that the nomination had been "a triumph for conservatism." Even Judah P. Benjamin and Robert Toombs, the outspoken representatives of the lower South, were reported to have expressed their surprise at Lincoln's moderation.

Because it was not customary for candidates for the highest office in the land to campaign actively, Lincoln did not deliver any important speeches during the race. But his supporters constantly argued about his commitment to antislavery principles. While appealing to potential conservative voters, they could reassure radicals with his record. The man who two years earlier had declared that a house divided against itself could not stand was clearly no friend of the hated institution. Had he not expressed his conviction that it would eventually disappear? "There is nothing in his speeches," the New Hampshire Republican Amos Tuck pointed out, "that encumbers us in our canvass, or serves to humble him, in comparison with our best men. It is marvelous to me, that such is the fact, when I observe the multiplicity of exigencies in which he has been placed, and how easy it would have been on many occasions to say an unnational, unwise thing."[1]

Lincoln's Initial Stance

When the election returns were in, the tug-of-war for the president's support began in earnest. Radicals insisted that he include Chase and other antislavery stalwarts in the cabinet. Conservatives like former Senator Truman Smith of Connecticut had other ideas. He had voted for Lincoln in the same way that he had voted for former Whig candidates, Smith wrote. His vote had been cast in the belief that the administration would be "moderate, impartial, just and conservative." Chase congratulated Lincoln on his election and "the overthrow of the Slave Power,"[2] while Raymond of the *New York Times* wanted him to make a statement assuaging the South. The president-elect, however, still refused to commit himself in public.

Lincoln's silence did not mean that he was unwilling to take a stand. When Congress began to consider various compromise proposals, he remained firm. "Let there be no compromise on the question of *extending* slavery," he wrote to Senator Trumbull of Illinois,[3] and he repeated this admonition to others. But at the same time, he informed Trumbull that he favored the enforcement of all laws, the Fugitive Slave Law among them. He also assured John A. Gilmer, the North Carolina Unionist, that he would favor the repeal of such state legislation as conflicted with the Fugitive Slave Act. To Raymond, who had sent him a letter from a Mississippian charging him with the advocacy of unqualified racial equality, he made an emphatic denial: he was neither pledged to the ultimate extinction of slavery, nor did he hold, without qualification, the black man to be the equal of the white. His attitude was best summed up in his letter to Alexander H. Stephens, soon to become vice-president of the Confederacy. Assuring the Georgian that he was not going to interfere with slavery in the South, he concluded: "You think slavery is *right* and ought to be extended; while we think it is *wrong* and ought to be restricted. That I suppose is the rub. It certainly is the only substantial difference between us."[4]

As the secession crisis deepened, Lincoln merely reiterated his stand. Concerning the various compromise proposals then under discussion, he maintained his inflexible opposition to any arrangement sanctioning the extension of human bondage. But "as to fugitive slaves, District of Columbia, slave trade, and whatever springs of the necessity that the institution is amongst us," he cared but little.[5] Accordingly, Congress submitted to the states a proposed amendment to the Constitution which would have prevented it from ever interfering with slavery where it existed.

Lincoln's own sympathies have long been a subject of controversy among historians. According to T. Harry Williams, an unbridgeable gap existed between the president and his radical critics (see Document 16). According to David Donald and his successors, the rift has been highly exaggerated (see Document 17). To be sure, Lincoln was often vexed by the extremist pressure he had to endure. But he never broke irrevocably with the radicals. When Raymond in his book, *Life and Public Services of Abraham Lincoln*, attributed to him complaints about the "Jacobinism" of Congress, the president objected to the use of the term. He could not remember using it, he wrote to the author, and he did not want it published. Lincoln maintained friendly relations with Sumner and other ultras, and as time went on he made it quite clear that the radicals' aims were not too different from his own. In the last analysis, as he told John Hay, though the radicals in Missouri were "the unhandiest devils in the world to deal with," they were nearer to him than the other side. Their faces were set "Zionwards."[6]

As events would show, it was precisely in dealing with the slavery question that the president would demonstrate his great political finesse. Satisfying neither the radicals who demanded immediate emancipation nor their conservative opponents who opposed any interference with slavery, he allowed the ultras to push him forward while permitting the stand-patters to hold him back. In this way, he remained master of the situation. When the time was ripe, he could and would choose the proper moment for any measure he might deem wise.

Because of his basic antislavery orientation, no matter how carefully Lincoln balanced conservative pressure against radical demands, he did not stand still. Never abandoning his early convictions, he gradually edged his way towards emancipation. The conservatives were able to cause delay, but they were not able to change his mind.

No matter how committed the president might have been to change in the long run, when war broke out, he was determined to bring about but one end: the restoration of the federal Union. This to him seemed to be the main issue of the war; its successful solution would decide the larger question of the feasibility of democratic government in general. Antislavery would have to be subordinated to this larger aim.

It was against this background that Lincoln's first inaugural address must be considered. When the president sought to reassure the South that it need have no apprehensions about its human property, he was merely reiterating a position he had long held. But before he finished writing the document, he took pains to show it to representatives of both factions. In February, Carl Schurz visited him at Springfield. Confiding to the German-American that he would show him a mark of trust that he had given to no one else, he ushered Schurz into a locked room where he kept the manuscript, then in preparation. "I shall never betray my principles and my friends," he said.[7] Then he showed the draft to his visitor. The radical leader was highly flattered.

Shortly afterwards, in Indianapolis, the president-elect also took his conservative friend Browning into his confidence. He even accepted Browning's advice to omit all references to his intention of reclaiming the public property and places which had fallen into the hands of the insurgents. The result was that both sides received the address favorably. Moreover, he took care to select a cabinet representative of all factions.

In the period between the inauguration and the firing upon Fort Sumter, the administration's chief problem was not slavery, but the question of the disposition of the federal forts in the South. Nevertheless, the issue remained crucial. In his famous April 1, 1861, proposal to the president, Secretary of State Seward suggested not only that the government adopt a positive policy, possibly including a foreign war, but also that it "change the question before the public from one upon slavery, for a question upon Union or disunion" (see Document 3). Although Lincoln rejected Seward's peculiar advice, he had already determined to pursue the domestic course the secretary advocated.

When war broke out twelve days later, the unprecedented patriotic uprising in the North confirmed Lincoln in his decision to appeal to the public to preserve the Union, rather than to launch a crusade for freedom (*Alternative 1:* see Document 3). The proclamation calling out 75,000 men to suppress rebellion did not mention slavery, although it carefully spelled out an injunction to the troops to avoid any interference with private property. The cautious policy of the preceding months was to be continued.

Yet from the very beginning, it was clear that civil war would eventually bring about changes. Many Republicans must have shared the opinion of James A. Hamilton, the son of the first secretary of the treasury. As long as the South remained faithful to the Union, Hamilton had not permitted himself to become an active opponent of slavery. As soon as the slave states threw off their allegiance and freed him from his constitutional obligations, however, he became "a most determined abolitionist."[8] Senator James R. Doolittle of Wisconsin, who had always hoped for a peaceful solution involving gradual emancipation coupled with colonization, now thought that "the madness of these fanatical traitors" was preparing a speedier solution "and that nearer home."[9] Charles Francis Adams, Lincoln's moderate minister to Great Britain, was convinced that slavery would have to be abolished. Even such practical Republicans as Isaac P. Christiancy of Michigan, not particularly known for radicalism, confessed to Governor Austin Blair that when Jefferson Davis was issuing letters of marque authorizing individuals to seize American ships, he wished to see the inauguration of war upon slavery.

Radical leaders were delighted. Thanks to the madness of the slave masters, James M. Ashley exulted, antislavery sentiment had grown more rapidly during the past thirty days than it had previously during the last thirty years. Sumner foresaw utter defeat for the insurgents and the extinction of slavery in blood, and Schurz told John Hay that thousands of Democrats were saying the time to remove the cause of the country's woes had come. "What we could not have done in many lifetimes," he asserted, "the madness and folly of the South have accomplished for us. Slavery offers itself more vulnerable to our attack than at any point in any century. . . ."[10]

It was clear to the radicals that Lincoln did not fully share their optimistic views. If they wanted to prevail, they would have to keep up their pressure, and they were not backward in doing so. Their chief spokesman in the cabinet was Secretary Chase, whom they considered one of their own. Calling Chase the only member of the cabinet able to bring the subject of emancipation to the president's attention, Giddings wrote to the secretary to urge the publication of an emancipation proclamation which would free the slaves in Virginia. Such a policy, Giddings asserted, would cripple the entire South because every able-bodied male would have to go home to look after the slaves to prevent rebellion. William F. Channing, the great Unitarian minister's son, explained to Chase that John Quincy Adams had always believed martial law could be used to effect emancipation. The first step ought to be martial law in the rebellious states; the second, emancipation by virtue of martial law; the third, an invitation to the loyal states to accept compensation for their slaves; the fourth, an appeal to non-slaveholding whites to sustain the government. And John Jay, the New York abolitionist, in a letter to Chase, suggested that Lincoln stress the antislavery theme in his forthcoming message to Congress. "It would enlighten the mind of Europe and the world at large." [11]

The radicals did not hesitate to go to Lincoln directly. In the presence of the secretary of the treasury, who was looking on with evident approval, James A. Hamilton read to the president a plan to free the slaves. When Schurz visited the White House on May 10, he voiced his antislavery opinions, and at the end of the month, Sumner raised his favorite subject while taking an evening's carriage ride with Lincoln. Conceding the justification for caution at the moment, the senator nevertheless asserted that the time would come when the president would have to strike at slavery. John Jay urged Lincoln to press for a confiscation act, and religious groups appealed to him "to proclaim liberty throughout the land." [12]

Conservative Pressures and Military Exigencies

Lincoln carefully evaded any direct response to these appeals. The situation, especially along the border, was still so fluid that he had to avoid any semblance of favoring emancipationist notions. Moreover, conservative pressure upon him was at least as potent as competing radical demands.

The importance of persisting in his conservative approach was brought home to the president the day after he delivered his inaugural address. Governor Edwin D. Morgan of New York, a moderate Republican, wrote that he could not let one day go by without expressing the satisfaction he felt at the message. "In common with many friends," he pointed out, "I have been trying for several years to bring this government back to the principles of the fathers. I now believe the *last* effort is a success." [13] And the hesitation of all but one of the members of his cabinet about holding Fort Sumter showed Lincoln that any radical step would cause great misgivings in the North. The New York *Herald* warned that if the radicals brought about coercion, they would be lynched in every Northern city.

This situation did not change after the firing upon Fort Sumter. The outbreak of war merely heightened the crisis in the border states. At a time when local authorities implored Lincoln not to send troops even through Maryland, a state which lay across the access routes to Washington, he could hardly countenance any interference with slavery. As it was, he was being asked by border state Unionists to render them assistance in returning fugitives to their owners.

In Kentucky, political conditions were even more ominous. Locked in a desperate struggle with Southern sympathizers, Unionists needed all the support they could muster from Washington. Imploring him to place himself on Henry Clay's platform, Lincoln's friends warned him that he must inform Congress that no crusade against slavery was intended.

What was true of Maryland and Kentucky was also true of Missouri. Fiercely rent by strife between secessionists and various Unionist factions, the state government was eventually superseded by a convention which deposed the secessionist governor and his assistants. But, as John S. Phelps insisted in a telegram to the president, Lincoln must beware of radicalism. "The Union party of this portion of the State are not free soilers," he pointed out. "Rashness and impudence may overwhelm us." [14]

Northern Democrats, too, warned the administration against radical actions. The government ought to be very careful to observe the Constitution, warned the Columbus *Crisis*. A movement to free the slaves would be "as base and rebellious as the conduct of Davis and his Confederates. It would be an open and avowed disregard of the Constitution." And the New York *Herald* expressed its satisfaction that the "disunion abolitionist fanatics of the school of Lovejoy, Sumner, and Pomeroy" were in a "contemptible minority." [15]

Under normal circumstances, Lincoln might simply have left well enough alone. But times were not normal. The exigencies of armed conflict hurried him on. It was impossible to wage war in a slaveholding area and not to make some decisions concerning the peculiar property in human beings, for this property was bound to affect military operations.

At first, in keeping with the administration's announced policies, military commanders in various areas sought to reassure slaveholders. On April 23, General Butler informed Governor Thomas H. Hicks of Maryland that he had not come to interfere with the domestic institutions of the state and that he was prepared to assist him in putting down slave uprisings. On May 14, General William S. Harney declared that the federal government would protect slave property in Missouri, and on May 26, General McClellan issued a similar proclamation in western Virginia. Announcing that there would be no interference with slaves, he promised to crush "with an iron hand" any insurrection against lawful masters. [16] But by that time, his policy was already becoming obsolete.

Forty-eight hours earlier, on May 24, 1861, one day after Virginia ratified her secession ordinance, General Butler at Fort Monroe at the tip of the peninsula in the Old Dominion, was confronted with the demand of an enemy commissioner under a flag of truce to surrender three fugitives who had come into his lines. Butler's previous offer to suppress revolts in Maryland had already caused a furore in the North, and this time the situation was different. To the argument that he was obliged to surrender the runaways, he could reply that Virginia had seceded; to the rejoinder that the United States considered the ordinance of secession null and void, he answered that this was true, but that the slaves in question had been used to aid the insurgent army in constructing fortifications; consequently he was keeping them as contraband of war. He then reported the incident to Winfield Scott, the commanding general. Although he did not use the word "contraband" in this dispatch, it was picked up by the newspapers and captured the imagination of the North. Major Theodore Winthrop, the New York novelist then serving on Butler's staff, was exaggerating when he wrote, "an epigram abolished slavery in the United States,"[17] but for the remainder of the war, the public applied the term "contrabands" to runaway blacks no matter what their condition.

The administration had to do something about the incident. When the cabinet discussed the matter on May 30, Postmaster General Blair supported the normally radical secretary of the treasury, so that Lincoln and his advisers decided to approve Butler's action (*Alternative 3*). "The Department is sensible to the embarrassments which must surround officers conducting military operations in a State by the laws of which Slavery is sanctioned," Secretary of War Cameron accordingly wrote to Butler. "The Government cannot recognize the rejection by any State of its Federal obligations, nor can it refuse the performance of Federal obligations resting upon itself. Among those Federal obligations, however, no one can be more important than that of suppressing ... armed combinations formed for the purpose of overthrowing its constitutional authority."[18]   Therefore, while still enjoining careful regard for personal property, the department ordered Butler to refrain from surrendering to alleged masters any persons coming within his lines. The question of their final disposition was to be reserved for future decision. The first blow against slavery had been struck.

Far-reaching as this decision eventually proved to be, its immediate effects were not as general as might be supposed. With the War Department's sanction, individual commanders in the field continued to enjoin their troops not to interfere with slavery, and on June 3, General Robert Patterson, advancing against Harper's Ferry, issued a proclamation to his forces cautioning them to protect private property and, if necessary, to suppress servile insurrection.

Butler himself had not been able to solve the slavery problem with his ingenious definition of runaways as contraband of war. What was to be done with women and children? More and more blacks entered his lines, and as he informed General Scott, the numbers he was holding were a matter of great importance to the enemy. As property alone, they were worth some $60,000. Nor could he well keep the males, whom he had usefully employed on the erection of batteries, and send their wives and children back into slavery. Requesting the advice of his superiors, he sent a copy of his report to the secretary of war. He would not receive a reply for several weeks to come.

Radical Pressure in Congress

When the special session of Congress met on July 4, Lincoln was again careful to inform the lawmakers that he had no revolutionary intentions (*Alternative 1*). "*[A]fter* the rebellion shall have been suppressed," he declared, "the Executive deems it proper to say, it will be his purpose then, as ever, to be guided by the Constitution, and the laws; and that he probably will have no different understanding of the powers, and duties of the Federal government, relatively to the rights of the States, and the people, under the Constitution, than that expressed in his inaugural address."[19] The word "probably", however, was significant. Changes might in fact come.

The mood of Congress could be gauged early in the session. Not only did the radical wing of the party secure a victory with the election of Galusha Grow as Speaker of the House, but on July 9, the House of Representatives passed a resolution declaring that the return of fugitive slaves was not part of the duties of a soldier of the United States. The Battle of Bull Run, however, with its revelation of federal unpreparedness, caused the conservatives to reassert themselves. Within a few days of the defeat, both Houses passed the Johnson-Crittenden resolutions declaring that it was not the purpose of the government to destroy the established institutions of the states, and that as soon as the supremacy of the Constitution and the inviolability of the Union had been vindicated the war ought to cease (see Document 4). As it was, conservative newspapers were blaming "rabid and reckless anti-slavery disorganizers" for both the war and the lost battle.[20] Lincoln was bound to take notice.

But the radicals were undaunted. "We need these reverses to bring people up to the peril of abolishing slavery,"[21] wrote K. S. Bingham of Michigan. John Jay agreed. Arguing that the time had come to draft and raise Negro troops, he suggested that authority be given to commanders to proclaim emancipation in their districts.

That Congress had not surrendered to the conservatives became clear with the passage of the first antislavery legislation to be adopted by the new majority. Confiscation bills had been pending in both houses before Bull Run. Afterwards, strengthened by the specific inclusion of slaves used in military operations against the government, the first Confiscation Bill was passed and presented to Lincoln for his signature.

The president was not happy with the measure. It was not that he disapproved of its provisions; as he had already told his friend Orville Browning on July 8, he agreed that the government neither should nor could send back fugitives who had come into federal lines. But he had grave misgivings about the timing of the bill. The Democratic press was already warning him that emancipation would disrupt the Union entirely; the border state situation was still very much on his mind (see Document 4), and, should he sign the legislation, he feared adverse effects particularly in Kentucky and Missouri.

Yet the necessity for some law could not be denied. Immediately after the Battle of Bull Run, Sumner saw the president again. Did Lincoln remember their previous conversation about slavery, the senator asked. The time for action had come. What the president said has not been recorded, although he could not fail to consider Sumner's views, especially since conditions in the field again required a speedy solution.

On July 30, the indefatigable General Butler again wrote to the secretary of war. As the number of slaves within his lines had greatly increased, he was still anxious to find an answer to the question of what was to be done with them. He suggested that they had been abandoned by their masters, and had thus become subject to their salvors, but as these did not recognize property in men, the Negroes were presumably now free. To some extent, the Confiscation Bill provided a solution.

Lincoln had to make a decision. If he vetoed the bill, conservatives would praise him and the position of border state Unionists would be strengthened. But there was a pressing military problem which the measure would ease. The proposed legislation was clearly justifiable, and there was the unmistakable majority in Congress which had passed it. The president signed the measure, and Cameron sent Butler an order approving his dispositions. The new act of Congress went far towards making the general's policy official (*Alternative 3*).

Lincoln's reluctant signature did not mean that he had chosen a single approach to the solution of the slavery question. Conditions in the border states, particularly in Missouri and Kentucky, were too unsettled to permit such an alternative. In Missouri, where General Nathaniel Lyon, the one man who more than any other had succeeded in routing the secessionists, had been killed in the Battle of Wilson's Creek, the federal army was under the command of General John C. Frémont. A popular but tactless leader, the general might easily antagonize conservative Unionists whose support was essential. As it was, he soon demonstrated his lack of military skill and began to quarrel with the powerful Blair family. At the same time, Kentucky was maintaining a precarious policy of neutrality. Any untoward move in Missouri or elsewhere might give the edge to local secessionists anxious to take the state out of the Union.

Keeping the Border States Loyal

It was at this juncture of affairs that General Frémont issued an order establishing martial law in Missouri and declaring the insurgents' slaves in the state free. Beset by difficulties, charged with his underlings' corruption, and threatened with military setbacks, he decided on this course after exposure to radical propaganda in order to strike at his enemies. Overnight, Frémont became a hero to radicals throughout the country. The moment they had been waiting for seemed to have arrived.

Lincoln, however, was not the man to surrender his ultimate power of deciding on a policy of dealing with slavery. Telegrams from Missouri and Kentucky warned of disaster unless he countermanded Frémont's order, and he was determined to sustain Unionists there if he possibly could. Consequently, disregarding the widespread support for Frémont, he made up his mind to revoke the order.

In view of the controversial nature of his decision, Lincoln was not willing to offend the general unnecessarily. In a polite letter, he asked Frémont to rephrase his edict to bring it into conformity with the Confiscation Act. Frémont refused. He even sent his wife Jessie, the redoubtable daughter of Senator Thomas Hart Benton, to Washington to plead his cause. But the president remained firm. Determined not to be thwarted in his effort to keep the border states loyal, he heeded the demands of Kentucky and Missouri Unionists and issued the revocation order himself. "I think to lose Kentucky is nearly the same as to lose the whole game," he wrote to Browning, who had sought to interfere in Frémont's behalf. "Kentucky gone, we cannot hold Missouri, nor, as I think, Maryland. These all against us, and the job on our hands is too large for us. We would as well consent to separation at once, including the surrender of this capital" (see Document 5).[22] Frémont was eventually recalled and conservatives rejoiced. But nothing had changed. The president was merely insisting that the responsibility for dealing with slavery was his.

Lincoln's caution paid dividends. Missouri did not secede, and, after the invasion of the state by a Confederate army, the neutrality of Kentucky soon came to an end.

Renewed Radical Pressure

The radicals were sorely disappointed at Lincoln's revocation of Frémont's order. Privately, they castigated the president in scathing terms; in public, their newspapers kept up the pressure for emancipation. The New York *Tribune* reiterated its opinion that slavery, the cause of the war, must be abolished; the New York *Evening Post* asserted that the president was lagging behind the people, the cabinet, Congress, and the military. On the last Thursday in September, which Lincoln had proclaimed a fast day, antislavery clergymen utilized the occasion to preach fiery sermons against the sin of holding human beings in bondage. And when Sumner addressed the Republican state convention at Worcester, Massachusetts, he asserted that the overthrow of slavery would at once put an end to the war. He believed that the dictates of military strategy, economy, common sense, and humanity all demanded that the federal government abolish the "peculiar institution."

Additional radical pressure upon the president followed the unfortunate engagement at Ball's Bluff, where his friend Senator Edward Baker of Oregon lost his life. Infuriated by the setback, Chandler, Trumbull, and Wade came to Washington to hurry the army into battle. Although for the moment they were chiefly concerned with military affairs, their hatred of slavery was well known. Lincoln would have to take their opinions into account.

The radical agitation assumed a new dimension on November 13, when John Cochrane, the New York Democrat who had long been apologetic of the South, delivered a stirring speech to his regiment at Washington in the presence of the secretary of war. "Soldiers . . . ," he admonished, "You have arms in your hands . . . for the purpose of exterminating an enemy unless he submits to law, order, and the Constitution. If he will not submit, explode everything that comes your way. . . . Take the slave by the hand, place a musket in it, and in God's name bid him strike for the liberty of the human race."[23] Enormous applause greeted this exhortation, and the presence of the secretary of war, who expressed his approval, seemed to make it official.

The president knew that in the long run he could not disregard these developments. But Democratic newspapers were still warning against the dangers of abolitionism, the moderate Springfield *Republican* agreed with them, and John J. Crittenden begged Lincoln to say nothing about slavery in his forthcoming message.

Lincoln reacted in a characteristic fashion. Adopting neither of the two alternatives presented to him, he had recourse to a third: colonization, and compensated, gradual emancipation in the border states (*Alternatives 4 and 6*).

In the president's mind, these two approaches were linked. Fully aware of the popular prejudice against free Negroes but equally convinced that something had to be done, he began to consider plans for the settlement of freedmen on the isthmus of Panama, where the Chiriqui Company had secured certain rights to the land and minerals. Consequently, he referred the matter to the secretary of the interior for study. Then, strengthened by the admonition of so conservative an advisor as the historian George Bancroft, who wrote that history would not forgive him if he failed to root out slavery, he sought to obtain the cooperation of the border states in initiating a policy of compensated emancipation.

Lincoln's chief contact in the matter was Delaware's lone Congressman, George P. Fisher. Hoping to secure the consent of the state legislature, the president gave Fisher two alternative drafts for a scheme of gradual abolition. According to the first draft, the United States would undertake to pay the state compensation to the amount of $719,200 in six percent federal bonds in five annual installments until after January 1, 1867, when all the slaves in Delaware would be free. The second plan was similar, except that payments would extend over a thirty-year period, until slavery would come to an end in 1893.

The president recurred to the problem in his annual message. Calling attention to the fact that Congress had already passed a Confiscation Act, he surmised that some of the states might wish to follow suit. He recommended that funds be appropriated for this purpose and again stressed his interest in colonization (*Alternatives 4 and 6*). The administration was evidently no longer so adamant about preserving the "peculiar institution."

Caution, however, was still necessary. Many of the generals in the field were Democrats; indeed, Lincoln had been careful to appoint members of the opposition party to high army posts. George B. McClellan, Don Carlos Buell, John Adams Dix, and Henry W. Halleck, to mention only a few, all sympathized with the conservatives. When campaigning on the eastern shore of Virginia, General Dix on November 2 issued a proclamation reassuring slaveholders that he would not disturb their property and that no runaways would be received within his lines. In Missouri, on November 20, Halleck issued General Order No. 3, which similarly kept fugitives out of his lines, and McClellan's parallel policies in Virginia had never been modified. In the midst of one war and threatened with another because of a diplomatic crisis with Great Britain following the seizure of Confederate agents aboard the British ship, the *Trent*, the president could ill afford to offend important segments of the army. He would have to maintain an equilibrium between radical insistence and conservative intransigence.

That the pendulum would not come to rest at dead center became evident as the year was drawing to a close. Congress was in no mood to turn back. Not only did it refuse to reaffirm the Johnson-Crittenden resolutions, but it began to consider a series of measures weakening the Southern labor system. Radicals introduced bills to abolish slavery in the District of Columbia and the territories, to repeal the Fugitive Slave Law, and to prohibit the return of fugitives by the army. In addition, it set up the Committee on the Conduct of the War, an agency which would soon become identified with radicalism.

The Joint Committee on the Conduct of the War was established early in the session as a result of a motion to investigate the disaster at Ball's Bluff. Charged with inquiring into "the conduct of the present war," it was chaired by Wade. Zachariah Chandler of Michigan, George W. Julian of Indiana, John Covode of Pennsylvania, and Daniel Gooch of Massachusetts were the other Republican members, while Andrew Johnson of Tennessee and Moses Odell of New York represented the Democratic minority.

The committee's activities soon became a matter of controversy. Summoning generals and other leading army figures to secret sessions, the investigators sought to ferret out laggards and imposters. As time went on, they became especially hostile to General McClellan. Frequently visiting the White House, they pressed Lincoln to substitute good Republicans for allegedly incompetent or unwilling Democrats. And they demanded that he abolish slavery as well.

The Committee's demand for emancipation did not take place in a vacuum. Secretary of War Cameron, beset by constant rumors of corruption and inefficiency in his department, began to espouse radical causes, possibly in order to save himself. During the fall, Union forces had captured the coastal districts of South Carolina in the vicinity of Beaufort, especially the Sea Islands from which virtually all the white inhabitants had fled. The large numbers of blacks who remained behind fell into federal hands, and it became necessary to devise some policy for dealing with them. Cameron now advocated their use for military purposes. Accordingly, he included in his annual report a section dealing with the subject. Asserting that the rebels' most valuable property was their claim to the labor of their slaves, he asked why this property should be exempted from the hazards of war. "If it shall be found that the men who have been held by rebels as slaves are capable of bearing arms and performing efficient military service," he concluded, it is the right, and may become the duty of this Government to arm and equip them, and employ their services against rebels. . . ."[24] Thus he fully endorsed Cochrane's proposal.

When discussing the secretaries' reports on December 2, Lincoln asked Cameron to modify his suggestions. The secretary did so, but he had already leaked his original recommendations to the press. In the resulting furore, Cameron was eventually eased out of office. Stanton became his successor. If anything, he was, or shortly would be, even more committed to antislavery measures than Cameron had ever been. Moreover, the president himself, shortly before the new year, told Sumner that the senator was ahead of him only by a month or six weeks. It was evident that events were favoring emancipation. The year 1862 would be one of decision.

Notes

1. Amos Tuck to David Davis, August 24, 1860, Robert Todd Lincoln Papers, Library of Congress, Washington, D.C.

2. Smith to Lincoln, November 7, 1860; Chase to Lincoln, November 7, 1860, Robert Todd Lincoln Papers.

3. Roy P. Basler, ed., *The Collected Works of Abraham Lincoln* (New Brunswick, N.J.: Rutgers University Press, 1853), vol. IV, pp. 149-51.

4. Ibid., p. 160.

5. Ibid., p. 183.

6. Tyler Dennett, ed., *Lincoln and the Civil War in the Diaries and Letters of John Hay* (New York: Dodd, Mead, and Co., 1939), p. 108; David Donald, *Devils Facing Zionwards,* in *Grant, Lee, Lincoln and the Radicals: Essays in Civil War Leadership,* ed., Grady McWhiney (Evanston, Ill.: Northwestern University Press, 1964), pp. 72-91.

7. Frederick Bancroft, ed., *Speeches, Correspondence and Political Papers of Carl Schurz* (New York: G.P. Putnam's Sons, 1913), vol. I, pp. 179-80.

8. James A. Hamilton, *Reminiscences of James A. Hamilton . . .* (New York, 1869), p. 441.

9. Doolittle to Lincoln, April 18, 1861, Robert Todd Lincoln Papers.

10. Dennett, *Diaries of John Hay,* p. 22.

11. Jay to Chase, June 4, 1861, Chase Papers, Library of Congress, Washington, D.C.

12. Congregational Church Ministers et al., to Lincoln, June 6, 1861, Robert Todd Lincoln Papers.

13. Morgan to Lincoln, March 5, 1861, Robert Todd Lincoln Papers.

14. J.S. Phelps to Lincoln, June 3, 1861, Robert Todd Lincoln Papers.

15. Columbus *Crisis,* June 27, 1861; New York *Herald,* July 18, 1861.

16. Edward McPherson, ed., *The Political History of the United States of America During the Great Rebellion* (Washington, 1865), p. 244.

17. Theodore Winthrop, *Life in the Open Air and Other Papers* (New York, 1876), p. 293.

18. *The War of the Rebellion: . . . Official Records of the Union and Confederate Armies* (Washington: Government Printing Office, 1880-1901), series III, vol. I, p. 243. (Hereafter referred to as *O.R.*)

19. Basler, *Collected Works,* vol. IV, p. 439.

20. New York *Herald,* July 23, 1861.

21. K.S. Bingham to Jacob M. Howard, July 26, 1861, Howard Papers, Detroit Public Library, Detroit, Michigan.

22. Basler, *Collected Works,* vol. IV, pp. 531-33.

23. McPherson, *The Political History, Rebellion,* pp. 414-16.

24. Ibid., p. 249.

3

Towards the Emancipation Proclamation

When, in December of 1861, Lincoln told Sumner that he was only behind the senator a month or six weeks in his attitude towards slavery, he was not far from wrong. With the problem of the blacks constantly on his mind, he continued to weigh all available alternatives. Favorably disposed towards emancipation, he nevertheless knew that he still had to be very careful. Any untoward move, any premature step, might precipitate such calamities in the border states and among Northern Democrats that the consequences would be incalculable. Given the existing widespread anti-Negro prejudice, the problem of sustaining the North's will to fight could not be disregarded.

Nor was the slavery issue Lincoln's chief concern during the winter of 1861-62. Military problems took up most of his time, for the war was not going well. The Army of the Potomac did not move forward; General McClellan seemed at times downright insubordinate, and the administration was anxious to secure a quick victory which it was still hoping would end the war forthwith.

The pressure to strike at the "peculiar institution" in some way, however, did not let up. Ever since the opening of Congress early in December, various measures to weaken slavery and to improve the lot of the blacks had been introduced in both Houses. Bills to forbid the return of fugitives by the army, to end the use of the District of Columbia jail for the confinement of runaways, to abolish slavery in the District of Columbia, and to confiscate rebel property, engaged the attention of the lawmakers. Congress also began consideration of Lincoln's recommendation to establish diplomatic relations with the Negro republics of Haiti and Liberia, and by March, a new article of war prohibiting the return of fugitive slaves had become law. Radical strength was increasing, and Lincoln was not unaware of this fact.

The Committee on the Conduct of the War remained one of the main sources of radical pressure. In frequent interviews with the president, its members attempted to goad the administration and the army on to battle, and as time went on, a regular tug of war developed between the law makers and General McClellan. Anxious to remain on good terms with Congress and as yet unwilling to dispense with his ranking general, Lincoln had to take the committee's views into consideration. And the members were as insistent on emancipation as upon the vigorous prosecution of the war.

The continued threat of foreign recognition of the Confederate States also remained troublesome for the president. The *Trent* affair had been resolved peacefully, but Confederate propaganda, especially in Great Britain and France, was still making headway. Antislavery measures would undoubtedly offset it; the Union could count on the sympathy of the worldwide reform movement. As the American consul in Bristol advised Lincoln on December 10, "The only antidote for their [the secessionists'] mischief, would be in the trusty anti-slavery men of the United States, dealing with the anti-slavery men of England, and the anti-slavery sentiment, which seems to be universal."[1] When Carl Schurz returned from Europe late in 1861, he stressed the same point. Freeing the slaves would win European support, he insisted. The Prince de Joinville went one step further. Warning the president that he had heard rumors of an intended Southern bid for diplomatic support by promising emancipation within twenty or thirty years, he pleaded for immediate emancipation. "The anti-slavery party in Europe has been the only one there to sustain the cause of the Union," he pointed out. "The feeling of repugnance to recognizing a slave confederacy has perhaps contributed more than anything to prevent Europe from interfering in your affairs."[2] In view of these facts, emancipation would keep Britain and France from extending recognition to the Confederacy. The French emperor's cousin, Prince Jerome Napoleon, was of the same opinion. Europe could not understand, he protested, why the Union hesitated to free the slaves. "*Cette lèpre d'esclavage*", he insisted, could no longer continue. It required a solution.[3] Strengthened by these considerations, the radicals' pressure was bound to affect the president's thinking.

But counterpressure never ceased. Fernando Wood, the New York Democratic leader who in 1861 had briefly flirted with secession, now assured Lincoln that the president's "highly patriotic and conservative course" met with the "hearty concurrence of the Democratic masses" in his state.[4] Democratic newspapers continued to insist that the war must not be changed into a struggle for emancipation, and border state legislatures still passed resolutions reaffirming their opposition to any federal interference with their domestic institutions. The president's ingenuity was severely taxed.

In view of the conflicting influences upon him, Lincoln moved forward slowly. True, in February he refused to commute the death sentence meted out to Nathaniel Gordon, the convicted captain of a ship engaged in the African slave trade. Gordon was hanged after receiving a two weeks' stay of execution and thus became the first American to suffer the supreme penalty for the crime of trafficking in human beings. But further steps had to await a more propitious time.

By the beginning of March, 1862, the general outlook had somewhat improved. The victories in the west, especially the capture of Forts Henry and Donelson, had greatly uplifted Northern morale, and new vigor had been infused into the War Department by its new chief, Secretary Stanton. Against this background, Lincoln decided once more to turn to the problem of slavery.

Urging the Border States Towards
Compensated Emancipation

The president was now prepared to move further than ever before. Early in March, an emancipation meeting had been called to assemble in New York. At first, it looked as if the organizers would oppose the administration. But Lincoln, informed of the impending affair by Carl Schurz, asked to read the main speech beforehand. It advocated emancipation in the District of Columbia, confiscation of the insurgents' slaves, and compensation to loyal slave owners. The president expressed his approval, and on the day of the meeting, instead of showing hostility to the government, Sumner was told, people talked as if the gathering had been "an out and out administration affair."[5]

It was not merely Lincoln's prior approval of their speeches which reconciled the New York emancipationists to his policies. On March 6, fully accepting neither the radicals' militant demands nor the conservatives' cautious warnings, the president returned to his favorite policy of gradual compensated emancipation in the border states (*Alternatives 3 and 4*: see Document 6). In a message recommending that Congress adopt a joint resolution pledging financial aid to any state adopting the program, he forcefully pointed out its advantages. Since the insurgents' expectations rested upon the ultimate recognition of the independence of at least part of the disaffected region, they were sanguine that the loyal slave states would then become discouraged and join the South. "To deprive them of this hope," he asserted, "substantially ends the rebellion." Conceding that gradual emancipation was preferable to sudden abolition, he appealed to the lawmakers to compare the cost of the war with the infinitely smaller expense of paying for the freeing of the bondsmen in any particular state.

The message undoubtedly expressed Lincoln's true sentiments at the time. The reaction of the border states to any antislavery measure always worried him; if these communities were themselves to initiate steps toward emancipation, his problems would be greatly simplified. But to convince them of the necessity for action was not easy.

Lincoln tried his best to induce the border states to adopt his suggestions. Four days after he had sent his message to Congress, he met with representatives from the affected region. Cordially welcoming them, he assured his visitors of his goodwill. His message, he insisted, had been merely an attempt to assist them. Then he cleverly made use of radical pressure to spur on his conservative audience. To objections that the New York *Tribune* seemed to entertain different views about the message, he replied that he must not be expected to quarrel prematurely with the radical newspaper; indeed, he hoped never to have to do so. Thus he declined suggestions that his views as expressed in the interview be published. Fearing that an altercation with the "Greeley faction," as he called it, was impending, Lincoln's wish was to postpone an encounter until the time was right, or to avoid a clash altogether, if possible. He sought to dispel objections to the scheme's constitutionality—he had carefully examined the question, he said—and the meeting ended in apparent harmony.[6]

At first, the reception of the message was encouraging. Congress took up the president's suggestions, passed the appropriate resolutions, and set up a select committee. Northern states passed resolutions of support. The conservative Albany *Evening Journal* endorsed it; the *New York Times* was enthusiastic, and the New York *Herald*, after first criticizing it, finally maintained that everybody but the radicals was satisfied with Lincoln. Even Greeley had no substantial objections. It did not matter if the Columbus *Crisis* disapproved. The paper was the organ of the extreme peace Democrats and could not be expected to acquiesce (see Document 7).

The initial reaction in the border states was not wholly negative. Governor Hicks of Maryland, a slaveholder himself, took the trouble of thanking the president for his "patriotic, sensible, and prudent message."[7] The state's Union convention endorsed the plan, and the Missouri convention passed resolutions placing the matter before the public for consideration. Although in the long run none of the border states proved amenable to Lincoln's plan, a beginning seemed to have been made.

In Europe, too, the first effect was good. "The late message of the President on the subject of 'Compensated abolition' has given much pleasure here to all the friends of the United States," John Bright wrote to Bancroft.[8] The letter found its way into Lincoln's papers.

Increased and Effective Radical Pressure

In the meantime, radical pressure continued. On March 14, the abolitionist orator Wendell Phillips was received on the Senate floor. Introduced by Charles Sumner, the Boston firebrand received the personal attention of Vice-President Hamlin, who left his chair to welcome him. Abolitionist petitions arrived constantly at the White House, and the secretary of state concluded a treaty with Great Britain to suppress the international slave trade. The radical trend was so marked that Rudolf Schleiden, the minister of the Hanseatic Republic of Bremen, reported it to his superiors. Senators Sumner and Wade had told him, he wrote, that they expected no end of the war without complete emancipation. Although Democratic newspapers complained, and Attorney General Bates made it his special business to warn Lincoln to stand firm both against the radicals and the timid border state men in relation to the slave question, the president continued to move slowly but surely toward a policy of emancipation.

The clearest sign of things to come was the success of the bill which freed the slaves in the District of Columbia. Congress possessed the constitutional power to legislate on all subjects in the federal district, but heretofore it had been deemed unwise to interfere with slavery in Washington as long as it was legal in neighboring Maryland and Virginia. But the war and its attendant reforming zeal rendered these considerations nugatory, and after considerable debate, both Houses, against violent conservative opposition, passed the requisite legislation. Providing for a payment of a maximum of $300 per slave, the measure also earmarked a sum of $100,000 to assist those freedmen who desired to emigrate. On April 16, the president signed the bill and sent Congress a message expressing his satisfaction. He was especially gratified that the two principles of compensation and colonization were both recognized. Except for inveterate conservative opinions, national reaction to the reform was generally favorable.

The momentum provided by these developments continued. Congress passed legislation ending slavery in the territories, providing for the education of blacks in the District of Columbia, and recognizing Haiti and Liberia. It also began debate on the second Confiscation Act, a most thoroughgoing measure which included provisions not only for the emancipation of the insurgents' slaves, but also for the enrollment of blacks in the federal army. Lincoln signed all these bills. In spite of his objections to some of the features of the Confiscation Act—he refused to assent to it until its operation had been limited to the natural life of the individual offender—eventually he also gave it his approval. It was evident that matters were moving toward a climax.

For one thing, the abolitionists' propaganda constantly increased. Petitions to end slavery continued to pile up on Lincoln's desk; Sumner delivered fiery speeches against the "peculiar institution" in the Senate, and newspapers and periodicals kept up the agitation for war against slavery. With great interest, the nation watched developments on the Sea Islands in South Carolina, where blacks were engaged in an experiment to run their fugitive masters' estates. Carried out under the aegis of the secretary of the treasury, the experiment provided Chase with new arguments to press his emancipationist views in the cabinet.

But the president was still not ready to move too far or too fast. He proved this when the commanding general of the Department of the South, David Hunter, took matters into his own hands. Declaring that martial law and slavery in a free country were incompatible, on May 9, Hunter announced that all slaves in Georgia, Florida, and South Carolina were henceforth forever free. He was already arming some of them with the secret support of the secretary of war.

Hunter was following the policy of emancipation by commanding generals in the field which Chase and others had long advocated. Although the secretary of the treasury had an appointment in Philadelphia at the time Lincoln was considering Hunter's proclamation, he did not allow the opportunity to pass without pleading for his favorite scheme. "It seems to me of the highest importance," he wrote to Lincoln, "whether our relations at home or abroad are considered, that this order not be revoked. It has been made as a military measure to meet a military exigency, and should, in my judgment be suffered to stand upon the responsibility of the Commanding General who made it."[9] Schurz also urged Lincoln to sustain the general. While conceding that the order was a bit premature, he predicted that within a month or so such measures would become most natural. If the president endorsed it, people would readily acquiesce in the proclamation.

But Lincoln had different ideas. Unlike Chase and Schurz, he had to consider the conservatives' opinion as well as that of the radicals. Ex-Senator Reverdy Johnson of Maryland implored him to revoke the order; border state citizens were appealing to him to protect their constitutional rights; Northern moderates also protested. Moreover, Lincoln himself approved neither of Hunter's method nor timing, and he had no intention of surrendering his ultimate authority over a subject as crucial as the abolition of slavery. "No commanding general shall do such a thing, upon *my* responsibility, without consulting me," he pointed out to Chase.[10]

Under these circumstances, the president determined to countermand Hunter's policy. Accordingly, on May 19, he not only issued a proclamation revoking the general's order, but stated specifically that he reserved to himself the responsibility of deciding whether as commander-in-chief of the army and navy he possessed the authority necessary to emancipate the slaves. In addition, once more appealing to the border states to accept his suggestion of compensated emancipation, he reminded them of his message to Congress on the subject. "To the people of these States," he wrote, "I now earnestly appeal—I do not argue—I beseech you to make the argument for yourselves— you cannot, if you would, be blind to the signs of the times. . . . This proposal makes common cause for a common object. . . . The changes it contemplates would come gently as the dews of Heaven, not rending or wrecking anything. Will you not embrace it?"[11]

The reaction to Lincoln's revocation of Hunter's orders was much as expected. The radicals deplored it; the moderates and the conservatives applauded it. But the president did not break with the radicals. Sumner especially realized that the setback was only temporary. "Could you—as has been my privilege often—have seen the President while considering the great questions on which he has already acted, beginning with the invitation to emancipation in the States, then Emancipation in the District of Columbia, and the acknowledgment of the independence of Hayti and Liberia," he wrote on June 5 for publication in the Boston newspapers, "even your zeal would be satisfied, for you would feel the sincerity of his purpose to do what he can to carry forward the principles of the Declaration of Independence."[12] The senator had read Lincoln's mind correctly. He was only awaiting the right moment to act.

The Need For an Emancipation Policy

As the summer of 1862 was approaching, the president was again confronted with the slavery question. In the first place, the long-awaited peninsular campaign to capture the confederate capital had not been successful. At its conclusion, General McClellan had sustained heavy losses, and was further away from Richmond than at its beginning. Apparently the war was going to last longer than anyone had suspected; new weapons to defeat the rebels were called for, and a crusade against slavery might be the answer to the problem. In addition, the foreign situation had not improved. Talk of diplomatic recognition of the Confederacy continued, and both Great Britain and France would soon feel an acute shortage of their cotton supply, a contingency hitherto avoided because of the glut of cotton on the European market at the time of the outbreak of the war. In addition, the army was encountering more and more difficulty with the slave problem in occupied areas. In Louisiana, where after Admiral Farragut's brilliant capture of New Orleans, General Butler had occupied the city and the surrounding area, "the peculiar institution" caused trouble from the start. John W. Phelps of Vermont, one of Butler's generals and a convinced abolitionist, began to encourage runaways to come into his lines. Upon receiving complaints from local slave owners, Butler referred the matter to the cabinet. Some decision would have to be made. Elsewhere, too, runaways posed problems for local commanders, and it was becoming ever more apparent that blacks constituted not only a vast pool of manpower, but an excellent source of military intelligence as well. As General O. M. Mitchel, a Kentuckian in the Army of the Ohio, wrote to Stanton from Alabama, "The negroes are our only friends, and in two instances I owe my safety to their faithfulness."[13] He demanded that they be granted federal protection.

Finally, the clamor for an emancipation policy, both in and out of Congress, was still growing. Delegations visited the White House to plead for the abolition of slavery; radicals delivered fervent speeches, and the second Confiscation Bill slowly made its way through both Houses.

Nevertheless, Lincoln could not simply disregard the factors which had, ever since his inauguration, militated against freeing the slaves. He would still have to be very cautious, especially since 1862 was a mid-term election year. Emancipation would provide the Democrats with an excellent campaign issue against the administration, and in view of McClellan's lack of success, the border states were not secure by any means. Moreover, the conservatives never ceased their campaign of pressure upon the president.

The focus of the conservatives' attack was the pending Confiscation Bill. Since the confiscation of insurgent property included the seizure and emancipation of rebels' slaves, the measure became identified with radicalism from its inception. John J. Crittenden was selected to deliver a speech against the bill and emancipation in the House; Garrett Davis did the same in the Senate, and even moderate Republicans had qualms about it.

The president's reaction to the bill naturally became a matter of crucial importance. Because his veto was the conservatives' chief hope, they employed every method to influence his decision in their favor. His friend Orville Browning implored him to disallow it; according to the Illinois senator, a veto would result in a storm of enthusiasm in the border states, while contrary action would make it impossible for Unionists to sustain themselves there. Old Thomas Ewing, former secretary of the treasury and secretary of the interior, agreed. In a letter to Lincoln, he asserted that the measure reminded him of the atrocities committed by the ancient Persians, by Oliver Cromwell, and by the Spaniards, and suggested the possibility that a new party of the center be set up to counteract the radicals' influence. Finally, General McClellan, more conservative than ever, flatly came out against any innovations. In his famous letter from Harrison's Landing, he informed Lincoln that the president must assume responsibility for the overall civil and military policy of the government. The war, he warned, must be conducted "upon the highest principles known to Christian civilization. . . . Neither confiscation of property . . . or forcible abolition of slavery should be contemplated for a moment" (see Document 8). What he might do in case his advice was not heeded was an open question.

Confronted with this situation, the president carefully searched for a workable policy. Rejecting the alternatives of standing still or freeing all slaves at once, he arrived at a middle solution (*Alternative 3*). By relying on his authority as commander-in-chief of the army and navy in times of actual armed rebellion, Lincoln could circumvent the constitutional prohibition against federal interference with "the peculiar institution" in the states; by freeing only slaves in those areas still in rebellion within a specified period of time, he could avoid interfering with the rights of private property in the border states, and by framing a proclamation rather than allowing events to take their course, he could appeal specifically to the antislavery feeling of foreign nations. It was a brilliant way out.

Precisely when the president first drew up his emancipation proclamation cannot be determined. Years later, Major Eckart, who was supervisor of military telegraphs at the time, remembered that Lincoln made daily trips to the War Department Telegraph Office in June, "after McClellan's 'Seven Days' Fight."[14] Since that engagement did not end until the beginning of July, the major's memory was obviously playing tricks on him. Nevertheless, according to Hannibal Hamlin's grandson, Lincoln informed the vice-president of his plan as early as June 18. On that day, as Hamlin was about to leave for his home in Maine, the president took him to the Soldiers' Home, ushered him into the library, and locked the door. Then Lincoln told him that he had finally heeded his advice to free the slaves and read him a paper which he had drawn up. Hamlin was fully satisfied.

Apparently, then, the president prepared his proclamation, or at least its original version, sometime in June, 1862. In the course of his frequent trips to the War Department Telegraph Office, he asked Major Eckart for paper because he wanted to write something special. Then for a number of days he slowly composed a document at the major's desk. At the end of each day, he invariably requested that his notes be locked up. At first Eckart did not know it, but the president, acting alone and without cabinet advice, was drawing up the first draft of the Preliminary Emancipation Proclamation. Its publication, however, would have to await the right moment.

Indeed, the president was not yet ready to make the document public, or even to show it to his cabinet. In Congress, the debates over the Confiscation Bill revealed deep fissures within the Republican party, to say nothing of the Democratic opposition. The progress of the Seven Days' campaign caused Lincoln deep anguish, and the border states had failed to act upon his recommendation of gradual compensated emancipation.

By the end of June, new pressures had to be considered. McClellan's lack of success was becoming apparent, and his accusations that the administration was responsible for his plight were not calculated to dispel the general gloom. The exigencies of war made clear the requirement of more manpower, so that on July 1, Lincoln asked the governors for three hundred thousand additional volunteers. With manpower considerations of such importance, the president's thinking was bound to be influenced in favor of the utilization of black troops. Governor Francis H. Pierpoint of the Restored Government of Virginia was already complaining that McClellan's soldiers were working in the hot sun on entrenchments before Richmond. The rebels' slaves ought to be used for this purpose, he advised, and the soldiers spared for fighting. When the governor of a slave state made such suggestions, the president might well consider the advantages of tapping the black manpower pool.

Lincoln Selects an Alternative

Lincoln made his decision following his trip to the peninsula to visit McClellan and the Army of the Potomac. After conferring with the general and receiving the Harrison's Landing letter from him, the president came to the conclusion that something drastic must be done. But before committing himself, he tried once more to win over the border states to his way of thinking.

The representatives of the loyal slave states came to the White House on July 12. "Gentlemen," the president said to them, "After the adjournment of Congress, now very near, I shall have no opportunity of seeing you for several months. Believing that you of the border-states hold more power for good than any other equal number of members, I feel it a duty ... to make this appeal to you. I intend no reproach or complaint when I assure you that in my opinion, if you all had voted for the resolution in the gradual emancipation message of last March, the war would now be substantially ended." His plan could still be adopted, he continued. If the border states waited too long, the institution of slavery would die anyway. Then he again used the radicals to spur on the conservatives. General Hunter, he said was an honest man, and in repudiating the general's proclamation, he had given offense to many whose support he could not afford to lose. "By conceding what I ask now," he pleaded, "you can relieve me, and much more, can relieve the country, in this important point (*Alternative 4*)."[15]

Although Lincoln tried once more to win over Congress to his preferred plan by sending it the draft of a bill to carry out his suggestions, his exhortations remained unheeded. Within two days, the majority of his visitors, reminding him of the promises given in his inaugural address, refused to consider his proposals. Every state had the right to hold slaves, they responded, and while they were willing to vote money and men to suppress the rebellion, antislavery measures would only unify the South against them. His last effort to induce the border to change had failed.

Apparently sensing the futility of his effort, Lincoln did not even await the border states representatives' reply before taking up his proclamation with members of the cabinet. On July 13, while riding in a carriage with Seward and Welles on the way to the funeral of one of Stanton's children, he mentioned the subject. Emphasizing the importance of the decision, he said that he had given it much thought and had come to the conclusion that it was a military necessity essential for the salvation of the Union. The secretaries replied that they would think the matter over.

The climax came during the second half of July. Although the president signed the Confiscation Bill, he infuriated the radicals by transmitting to Congress the veto message he would have sent had his demands for certain changes been disregarded. In the Senate, Zachariah Chandler delivered a violent diatribe against McClellan which was widely interpreted as an attack on the administration, and when Congress adjourned, the radicals issued an address which once more demanded the abolition of slavery. But Lincoln was already preparing to put his own antislavery policy into action. "The Slavery question perplexes the President almost as much as ever and yet I think he is about to emerge from the obscurities where he has been groping into somewhat clearer light," Chase confided to his friend R.C. Parsons on July 20. Then he mentioned Lincoln's plan to "enfranchise" the slaves of all rebels unless they returned to their allegiance within sixty days.[16]

Whether the date of Chase's letter was incorrect or whether he had prior knowledge of what would transpire within the next forty-eight hours is not known. At any rate, after the adjournment of Congress, on July 21, Lincoln told his cabinet that he had been deeply concerned about the current aspect of affairs. As a result, he had prepared several orders. The first was an authorization to commanders to allow their troops to subsist in hostile territory. The second conferred authority upon them to employ Negroes as laborers. The third provided for a strict keeping of accounts of seized property, and a fourth, for the voluntary colonization of blacks in some tropical country (*Alternative 6*). The secretaries generally consented. Stanton submitted another request from Hunter for black troops, but Lincoln was not yet ready to go that far.

On the next day, the cabinet met again. Unanimously agreeing to drop the colonization order, it turned to the others, which were approved. When the possibility of arming the blacks was brought up, Chase supported it warmly. Lincoln, however, again rejected the proposal, at least for the time being. Instead, he produced the Emancipation Proclamation which he had written. Based upon the Confiscation Act, it called upon the insurgent states to return to their allegiance to the Union. Otherwise, the provisions of the law would go into full effect after sixty days, and Lincoln himself would issue a proclamation freeing all slaves remaining in insurgent states on January 1, 1863 (*Alternative 3:* see Document 9).

At this important meeting, all the secretaries were present. Blair arrived late. When Lincoln informed them that he had made up his mind, all but the postmaster general agreed with his decision, although Chase still preferred individual action by commanders in the field. According to the account which Lincoln later gave to both Congressman Owen Lovejoy and the painter Francis B. Carpenter—a version generally accepted by Welles after the war—Seward then suggested that the proclamation be postponed until the military situation looked more promising. Otherwise, he was afraid that it would be considered "our last shriek, on the retreat (*Alternative 7*)." Lincoln took the various objections into consideration, and the meeting adjourned (see Document 10).

That afternoon, for the second time in two days, the president met with the conservative New York Democrat, Francis Brockholst Cutting. Stanton had sent Cutting to Lincoln on the previous day because the New Yorker was now in favor of emancipation. Later that night Seward's friend Thurlow Weed counseled delay, and Lincoln postponed the date of the issuance of the proclamation. Whether he took this action because of Seward's and Weed's arguments or because of Chase's hesitation, as Benjamin P. Thomas and Harold M. Hyman have suggested (see Document 21), is difficult to determine. Whatever the reasons for the delay, however, he had taken the first steps towards freedom.

In deciding upon this particular way of freeing the slaves, Lincoln had once more given proof of his skill as a politician. Urged by radicals and foreign observers to emancipate immediately and unconditionally, warned by conservatives to stand pat, he chose the middle way. Keeping in mind the state of the country, the military situation, his constitutional prerogatives as commander-in-chief, and the endemic racial prejudice of his fellow citizens, he arrived at a viable solution. Moreover, instead of following Chase's advice to permit local commanders to emancipate without fanfare, he decided to issue a specific proclamation (*Alternative 3:* see Documents 9 and 10). He was not the man to overlook the propaganda effect of such action in foreign countries. Thus he selected the one alternative most likely to lead to success. All that remained was to find the right time for its implementation (see Documents 18, 19, and 21).

Notes

1. Zebina Eastman to Lincoln, December 10, 1861, Robert Todd Lincoln Papers, Library of Congress, Washington, D.C.

2. Prince de Joinville to Lincoln, February 8, 1862, Robert Todd Lincoln Papers.

3. Jerome Bonaparte to Edward Everett, February 18, 1862, Robert Todd Lincoln Papers.

4. Fernando Wood to Lincoln, January 15, 1862, Robert Todd Lincoln Papers.

5. Frank W. Ballard to Sumner, March 7, 1862, Charles Sumner Papers, Harvard University, Cambridge, Massachusetts.

6. Edward McPherson, ed., *The Political History of the United States of America During the Great Rebellion* (Washington, 1865), p. 211.

7. Hicks to Lincoln, March 18, 1862, Robert Todd Lincoln Papers.

8. John Bright to Bancroft, March 29, 1862, Robert Todd Lincoln Papers.

9. Chase to Lincoln, May 16, 1862, Robert Todd Lincoln Papers.

10. Roy P. Basler, ed., *The Collected Works of Abraham Lincoln* (New Brunswick, N.J.: Rutgers University Press, 1953), vol. V, p. 219.

11. Ibid., p. 223.

12. Charles Sumner, *The Works of Charles Sumner* (Boston, 1870-83), vol. VI, p. 116.

13. *O.R.*, series I, vol. X, part II, pp. 162-63.

14. David Homer Bates, *Lincoln in the Telegraph Office* (New York: The Century Co., 1907), p. 138.

15. Basler, *Collected Works*, vol. V, pp. 317-19.

16. Chase to R.C. Parsons, July 20, 1862, Chase Papers, Historical Society of Pennsylvania, Philadelphia, Pennsylvania.

The Decision

Once he had decided to emancipate the slaves in enemy-held territories, Lincoln still retained several options. He had yet to make up his mind about timing, the possibilities of black troops, colonization, and the method of implementation.

The problem of timing was of the utmost importance. How long was the decision to be kept secret? Was it to be implemented in the immediate future or was it to be put off indefinitely? Did it have to await a decisive victory or could it be announced as soon as federal military fortunes improved a little? Should it conform to the provisions of the Confiscation Act—freedom for rebels' slaves within sixty days—or should it be issued independently? Did it have to await the election results or could it be made public earlier? Lincoln would have to find some kind of answer to this conundrum.

The problem of the black soldiers would also have to be settled. According to the Confiscation and Militia Acts, the president possessed the right to employ Negro troops. He might or might not choose to exercise it. He might implement the law independently of the proclamation or in conjunction with it. He might utilize Negroes as noncombatants or as full-fledged soldiers. He might also let the whole matter rest, perhaps relying on individual generals to carry out the intent of Congress.

The question of colonization was frequently on Lincoln's mind. Public advocacy of black resettlement abroad would certainly lessen the opposition to emancipation. But how was colonization to be brought about? Voluntary cooperation of the blacks might be the answer. Whether this could be obtained, however, was doubtful.

The implementation of the decision also presented difficulties. Chase was still arguing for his plan of allowing local commanders to free the slaves. If the Treasury secretary's views were to prevail, Lincoln would have to scrap his proclamation, although the end effect might be the same. Since the foreign and domestic impact of a written document appealed to the president, however, it was unlikely that he would abandon his preference for a specific document issued by himself.

Finally, a decision would have to be made about the areas to be affected by the proclamation. Should it apply completely to all states in rebellion or should partial exemptions be made? Sooner or later, all these points would have to be resolved.

The general public was hardly aware of these problems. Generally uninformed about Lincoln's plans, radicals of all types kept up their pressure upon the administration. Even within the cabinet, agitation continued. Two days after the cabinet meeting on July 22, the New York Chamber of

Commerce passed resolutions calling upon the president to use emancipation as a weapon against the insurgents. On August 3, at another cabinet meeting, the Secretary of the Treasury, "for the tenth or twentieth time," to quote his own words,[1] urged his favorite scheme of emancipation by local military action, and on August 20, Horace Greeley published his famous "Prayer of Twenty Millions" in the New York *Tribune*. Asking the president to consider the fact that slavery everywhere was the exciting cause and sustaining base of treason, the editor called upon Lincoln to execute the Confiscation Act and declare the slaves of rebels forfeit (see Document 11). On September 7, ex-Governor George S. Boutwell of Massachusetts, then Commissioner of Internal Revenue, came to see the president on matters connected with his office. When at the end of the interview Lincoln asked him what he thought about McClellan, Boutwell replied that success depended on emancipation. On the same day, a public meeting in Chicago of Christians of all denominations adopted a memorial in favor of freedom for the slaves, a document presented to the president one week later. Moreover, Union governors were preparing to meet at Altoona, Pennsylvania, later in the month. It was an open secret that emancipation was one of their demands.

While these movements looking toward an end of slavery were impressive, military problems concerning the status of Southern blacks continued to plague the War Department. In Louisiana, General Phelps had gone so far as to enlist Negroes. When Butler disapproved, the abolitionist general submitted his resignation. Before long, however, Butler himself made plans to enroll a regiment of free blacks. Other generals soon followed suit.

Diplomatic difficulties also beset the administration. The repeated setbacks of Union armies strengthened pro-Confederate movements abroad, and Great Britain especially seemed to be edging closer to recognition of the Southern government. On July 18, Confederate sympathizer William Lindsay's motion for mediation was discussed in the House of Commons. Although it was not acted upon, when on August 4 Lincoln received news of the debate, he could hardly overlook the fact that friends of the Confederacy had cited his disallowance of Frémont's and Hunter's orders as proof of their contention that slavery was not an issue in the American Civil War. Long standing arguments for antislavery measures to prevent foreign interference were reinforced. The president must have become more convinced than ever that his idea of an official emancipation proclamation was much better than Chase's piecemeal plan.

Educating the Conservatives: Preparations for Emancipation

Nevertheless, in view of the various contending factions assailing him, Lincoln was still attempting to steer a cautious course. Painfully aware of the radicals' onslaught on the administration, the conservatives redoubled their efforts to keep the president from implementing their rivals' demands. Reverdy Johnson, the Maryland Union Democrat who had been sent to New

Orleans to investigate conditions there, angrily protested against General Phelps's policies. Lincoln's friend Speed, warning that Kentucky was on the brink of secession, asserted that the Negroes did not have the capacity to maintain their freedom even if it should be given to them. And on August 8, Edgar Cowan, the radicals' bitter antagonist in Pennsylvania, not only warned against emancipation but insisted that the radicals were "noisy zealots" responsible for all the nation's troubles.[2] Conservatives of all types implored the president to continue his evenhanded course, while representatives from the border states still sought his support against the emancipationists.

The harassed chief executive was hard pressed to find the proper course in maintaining some degree of unity in the government and country. The easiest way out seemed to be a renewed effort to stimulate the colonization movement. The Confiscation Act of 1862 had once again specifically authorized the president to make provisions for the voluntary settlement of freedmen in some tropical country beyond the borders of the United States. Postmaster General Blair, deeply worried about Lincoln's intention to publish an emancipation proclamation, redoubled his attempts to advance the movement, and various entrepreneurs offered to take charge of projects to settle freed blacks in Central America and the West Indies. But the Negroes' consent was essential, and the president now sought to obtain it (*Alternative 6*).

Lincoln's method was direct. After the commissioner of colonization, James Mitchell, who had long been active in the cause, had arranged for an interview, in the afternoon of August 14, the President received at the White House a Negro delegation headed by Edward M. Thompson. Mitchell introduced the visitors, and Lincoln asked them to be seated. Then he came straight to the point. A sum of money had been appropriated by Congress for the purpose of colonization, he said, and he desired to bring the subject to his guests' attention. Believing that a greater difference existed between the black and white races than between any others, he was of the opinion that the blacks for that reason suffered greatly by living among the whites, and the whites by the presence of the blacks. He considered slavery the greatest wrong inflicted on any people, but even when freed, the blacks would still not be equal to the whites. Thus, whether right or wrong, it would be best for both to be separated. Liberia was too far, but Panama might be just the place for colonization. If he could get a few black pioneers to start the project, he promised that he would give them every assistance. After asking for time to think the matter over, the delegation withdrew.

Although the proposal did not impress the black community, and although Lincoln probably foresaw its drawbacks from the start, he had nevertheless given a token of his goodwill towards the conservatives. Continuing to further colonization schemes, first at Chiriqui in Panama and then at the Île à Vache off Haiti, he made it easier for himself to proceed with his own plans for emancipation. That none of the projects ever succeeded made little difference.

In the meantime, the problem of the black troops continued to bedevil the administration. On August 4, a delegation of Westerners waited upon the president to offer two Negro regiments from Indiana. Although Congress had empowered the executive to employ black soldiers, the opposition of conservatives and border state politicians gave Lincoln pause. Nevertheless, he carefully sought to prepare public opinion for the steps he knew had to be taken.

Lincoln began his campaign for the education of conservatives with a reply to Reverdy Johnson's protest against the policies of General Phelps. The people of Louisiana, he wrote, knew full well the remedy for the general's presence: it was simply to take their place within the Union upon the old terms. But he concluded with a warning: "It may as well be understood, once and for all, that I shall not surrender this game leaving any available card unplayed."[3]

Two days later, the President wrote a similar letter to Cuthbert Bullitt, a Louisiana conservative who had also complained about military interference in the state. Let the Unionists establish a loyal government and the army could be withdrawn, he pointed out. For his part, he was going to do all he could to save the government. It was not beyond the realm of possibility that this "all" would include reliance upon black soldiers.

The president was not yet prepared to force the issue, however. When the western delegation offered him two regiments of black troops, he replied that he was not ready to go to the length of enlisting Negro soldiers. Arguing that the nation could not afford to lose Kentucky, he expressed the opinion that to arm the Negroes would turn fifty thousand bayonets from the border states against the Union. But he promised to employ all blacks offered as laborers.

Individual generals in the field took the next step. Although General Hunter's experiment with emancipating and arming Negroes had been disallowed, the secretary of war gave his blessing to similar efforts undertaken in the region by General Rufus Saxton. In Kansas, James H. Lane recruited Negroes, and in Louisiana, Butler finally armed a black regiment which had originally been called into service by the Confederates. The president did not interfere with any of these ventures.

Awaiting a Military Victory

Because of Seward's advice to await a favorable turn of the fortunes of war before announcing the emancipation policy, Lincoln was still forced to fend off attacks upon his hesitant course. When he received Greeley's "Prayer of the Twenty Millions," he might have disregarded it altogether, but he decided to meet the issue head-on. In a much-quoted public reply, he informed the editor and the country that it was his purpose to save the Union either with or without slavery. If he could save it only by freeing all the slaves, he would do it; if he could save it by freeing some, he would do that also; if he could only save it by freeing none at all, he would even do that. But lest he be misunderstood, he utilized the opportunity to assert once more his basic opposition to the "peculiar institution." "I have here stated my purpose according to my view of *official* duty," he concluded, "and I intend no modification of my oft-expressed *personal* wish that all men everywhere could be free" (see Document 11).

The delegation of Christians from Chicago received a similar answer. To their request that he carry out the will of Providence, the president replied that God had not revealed His will to himself, but that he would certainly carry it out if he heard it. Admitting that slavery was the root of the rebellion, that as commander-in-chief of the army he had the right to issue an emancipation proclamation, and that such a step would be helpful both in Europe and at home, he nevertheless pointed out that for the time being it would be somewhat ineffectual. But he ended on an optimistic note. "Do not misunderstand me . . . ," he said. "I have not decided against a proclamation of liberty to the slaves, but hold the matter under advisement . . . the subject is on my mind, by day and night, more than any other."[4]

Lincoln had not misled the Chicago delegation. Ever since July, he had been awaiting the proper time for his proclamation. But the military situation, far from improving, had become worse. After McClellan's failure before Richmond, John Pope launched an attack in Virginia, only to be defeated at the old battlefield of Bull Run. In desperation, Lincoln called once again upon McClellan to stem Lee's subsequent invasion of Maryland. Not until September 17 at Antietam, however, did the slow-moving commander of the Army of the Potomac succeed in inflicting something like a setback on the Southern forces. Lee recrossed the Potomac on the next day, and Lincoln was able to return to his long-dormant project (*Alternative 7:* see Document 10).

Whether the president reviewed all the options open to him after Antietam is not known. He said later that he had made a vow to issue the proclamation if Lee should be driven out of Maryland, and he probably considered the Southern reverse sufficient to justify the promulgation of his state paper. But during the days immediately preceding the final decision, a period which happened to correspond to the time limit imposed on the rebels in accordance with the Confiscation Act, he received additional pleas for action. Chief among these was a lengthy letter from Robert Dale Owen, endorsed by Chase, in which the British socialist's son pleaded eloquently for action. Pointing out that the end of the sixty days' grace granted by Congress was approaching, he argued that this circumstance provided the opportunity for immortal fame. One million men presently laboring for the South could just as well fight for the North. The chance to extirpate the great evil was at hand, wrote the reformer, who inclosed a proposed proclamation ending slavery throughout the United States. Chase gave the letter to Lincoln on September 20.

The Preliminary Proclamation

But the president had already made up his mind (*Alternative 3*). Busy drafting his proclamation on Sunday, September 21, he called a cabinet meeting for the next day. All the secretaries were able to attend.

Lincoln opened the meeting on a comic note. Reading Artemus Ward's "Highhanded Outrage at Utica," he permitted his advisors to relax. Then he became serious. "Gentlemen," he said, "I have, as you are aware, thought a great deal about the relation of this war to Slavery; and you all remember that, several weeks ago, I read to you an order I had prepared on the subject, which, on account of objections made by some of you, was not issued." Ever since that time, his mind had been much occupied with that subject. Now he thought the moment for action had come. Admitting that the success of the army in repulsing the enemy had not been as thorough as he would have liked, he nevertheless believed that it was sufficient for his purpose. "I have got you together to hear what I have written down," he continued. "I do not wish your advice about the main matter—for that I have determined for myself."[5] But he invited editorial suggestions, and, referring to the necessity for his taking responsibility for his decision, proceeded to read the proclamation.

In his careful wording of the Preliminary Emancipation Proclamation, Lincoln had finally chosen the one alternative that seemed most likely to assuage the radicals at home, please abolitionists abroad, and give rise to the least offense among conservatives in the border and loyal states (*Alternative 3:* see Document 12). By promising freedom to the slaves in areas still in insurrection on January 1, 1863, and by doing so specifically as president and commander-in-chief of the army and navy, he had clearly made the proclamation a war measure. In his capacity as commander-in-chief, he possessed the right to use whatever legitimate weapons of war were available. Since the end of slavery was one of these, he could and did promise bondsmen held by rebels that they would be "then, thenceforth, and forever free." By rejecting Chase's alternative of allowing local abolition of slavery, he obtained the maximum effect abroad; by refusing the conservatives' advice to do nothing (*Alternative 1*), he assuaged the radicals, and by not accepting radical demands for total emancipation (*Alternative 2*) he made it easier for conservatives and the border states to remain loyal. To allay the latters' fears further, he repeated his intention to continue waging the war for the purpose of restoring the Union, to persist in efforts to bring about compensated emancipation in the loyal states, and to seek ways of colonizing the freedmen. Moreover, for the time being, he did not mention the controversial issue of black troops (*Alternative 5*). The resulting proclamation was not a flaming manifesto—some abolitionists at home and abroad were disappointed with it—but it was a statesmanlike paper based on the options available to the president at the time.

By and large, the secretaries' reactions were favorable. Seward was the first to comment. "The general question having been decided," he remarked, "nothing further can be said about that." After proposing a few editorial changes, he advised that the voluntary nature of any contemplated colonization scheme be emphasized (*Alternative 6*).[6] Lincoln and the others substantially agreed, although Blair was still hesitant. While conceding that he had reluctantly come to approve of emancipation, the postmaster general thought the time was not ripe for it. His colleague Bates, who had previously advocated compensated emancipation, had no choice but to go along. The Preliminary Emancipation Proclamation was then put in final shape and sent to the printer (*Alternative 3:* see Document 12).

Once Lincoln had made and announced his decision, it might have been supposed that the problem was solved. But this was not the case. During the ensuing one hundred days, conservatives of all sorts sought to put pressure on the administration to renege on its promise, not to go through with the proclamation, and to allow the border states to pursue their own backward-looking course (*Alternative 8*).

The Hundred Days

The immediate reaction to the proclamation was not unfavorable. Despite the inevitable criticism from conservatives and ultras alike, the country accepted the document for what it was,—a necessary war measure. The border states did not secede. Many radicals, including Sumner, Wade, and Hamlin, enthusiastically endorsed the proclamation. The New York *Herald*, bitterly antiradical though it was, grudgingly approved of it. Administration organs like the Springfield *Republican*, stressing the diplomatic benefits to be expected from the new policy, pointed out the timeliness of the president's action, proof of his purpose to do nothing that did not lead to the salvation of the Union. While the immediate reaction abroad was not as friendly as had been expected because of the limited nature of the proposed reform, it was nevertheless clear that a Union victory would inevitably spell the doom of slavery throughout the United States.

In Washington, the aftermath of the announcement did not bring any great surprises. On September 24, the president, acknowledging the cheers of serenaders at the White House, admitted that he had made his decision after very careful deliberation. He expressed his trust in God that he had made no mistake and invited the country and the world to pass judgment on his action. The delighted Chase confessed his amazement at the insanity of the slaveholders. Had they stayed in the Union they might have preserved their institutions for years to come. But by seceding, they themselves had made it possible to destroy slavery. The president, welcoming the Northern governors who called on him shortly after the announcement, thanked them for their support of the proclamation. Their purpose, the government's endorsement of emancipation, had already been accomplished.

The first real test of the new policy came during the fall elections. Democratic newspapers and orators made the most of Lincoln's alleged breach of the Constitution. Candidates exploited the electorate's racial prejudices, and when the returns were in, it was clear that the administration's party had sustained serious losses.

Conservatives were jubilant. Asserting that the country had rejected the Emancipation Proclamation, they expressed hope that the president would reconsider. Had not the New York Republican Convention, meeting shortly after the publication of the proclamation, specifically endorsed it? Was it not certain that New York Republicans, like those in Ohio, Pennsylvania, Illinois, and elsewhere, had suffered severe losses? The Negro question was the "lever which moved the public mind," rejoiced the editor of the Columbus *Crisis*. He analyzed the election results as a firm popular expression against Ohio's becoming a depot for runaway slaves from the South.[7]

If conservatives hoped Lincoln would change his mind, they were mistaken. Determined not to let anything interfere with the vigorous prosecution of the war, a few days after the elections he removed General McClellan from command of the Army of the Potomac. The fact that the "Little Napoleon" was the Democrats' idol did not deter the president. And although he delivered no lengthy speeches about his antislavery policy, he told a visiting delegation of Kentucky Unionists that he would rather die than take back a word of the Emancipation Proclamation (*Alternative 9*).

Nevertheless, there were still a number of ways in which the emancipation policy could be made more palatable to conservatives. One of these was a continued pursuit of colonization, and Lincoln not only repeatedly discussed the idea with his cabinet, but actually proceeded to put it into practice (*Alternative 6:* see Document 13). At first he still attempted to carry out his plan to send a number of blacks to Chiriqui in Panama, but since Seward had found that the coal in the region was tertiary and therefore virtually worthless, the president's interest shifted to the Ile à Vache off Haiti. An adventurer named Bernard Kock succeeded in obtaining a contract for the settlement of freedmen there, and on December 31, one day before the projected promulgation of the final proclamation, the experiment finally received the president's blessing. He had already made certain to publicize colonization by prominently featuring it in his annual message.

In other ways, too, the president sought to soften the blow. When representatives from the border states visited him, he recurred to his notion of compensated emancipation (*Alternative 4*). He even devoted a significant part of his annual message to Congress to the subject. After briefly referring to the Emancipation Proclamation, he once more suggested a scheme to free the slaves gradually after paying for them. And so gradual was his plan that according to its provisions slavery would not come to an end until the year 1900. He could hardly go any further in his quest to appease the border states (see Document 13).

Either in spite of or perhaps because of these efforts to make emancipation palatable to the conservatives, speculation about the president's intentions mounted as the new year approached. Would he yield to the entreaties of border state Congressmen or would he remain firm? The final decision was up to Lincoln, but many politicians sought to influence him. And they still found various alternatives for him.

One of the spokesmen for the conservatives in the House was George Yeaman of Kentucky. Introducing a resolution condemning the proclamation as unconstitutional and not calculated to restore peace (*Alternative 8*), he brought it to a vote on December 11. It was overwhelmingly defeated, but he did not give up. As late as December 30, two days prior to the announced date of the final proclamation, he sent Lincoln a speech in which he reargued all the objections to a policy of freedom. His colleagues in the border states as well as Northern Democrats vigorously supported him.

Lincoln's friend Orville Browning also tried his best to dissuade him. In conversing with Judge Benjamin F. Thomas, a conservative Republican from Massachusetts, Browning suggested that Thomas seek an interview with the president to tell him that emancipation was extremely dangerous. It was fraught with evil and was bound to do much injury. If Lincoln was unwilling to withdraw the proclamation altogether, let him at least restrict it to slaves of insurgents in actual rebellion. Thomas saw the president during the last week of December. The pressure on the harassed chief executive never ceased.

But Lincoln could not be moved (*Alternative 9*). Not only did the passage of a resolution diametrically opposed to Yeaman's encourage him—he knew that he could count on a majority in the House—but reports from abroad also assured him that the proclamation would have a most salutary effect in Europe (see Document 14). Consequently, he held fast to his own convictions earlier expressed. As he told Sumner, he "could not stop the Proclamation if he would, and he would not if he could."[8] As the radicals kept insisting that his promises must be kept, he told Thomas, if he should refuse to issue the document, a rebellion would break out in the North, and a dictator would be placed over his head within a week.

If he had ever had any doubts about the intensity of radical feeling in Washington, the aftermath of the disastrous Battle of Fredericksburg once more reminded him of it. Spurred on by the radicals, a delegation of Republican senators demanded that he reorganize the cabinet. In an obvious attack upon Seward, who was suspect because of his conservatism, they proposed that only those believing in the vigorous prosecution of the war be included in the president's official family.

How Lincoln defeated this attempt to dictate the composition of his cabinet to him has often been recounted. When Seward submitted his resignation, the president resolved the crisis by inviting the senators to meet with his remaining advisers, including Chase, who had been one of the instigators of the revolt. The result was that the secretary of the treasury also offered his resignation, and Lincoln, rejecting both, reasserted his authority. But it was obvious that there was considerable sentiment for radical policies. The president was not going to change his mind about emancipation.

The Final Version: The Best Alternative

As the time for action approached, Lincoln devoted more and more time to the proclamation. On December 29, he read his proposed final document to the cabinet.

The document was even more skillfully worded than its predecessor. Citing the Preliminary Emancipation Proclamation, the president now proposed to carry it into execution. He carefully justified himself by relying on the powers vested in him as commander-in-chief of the army and navy of the

United States in time of actual armed rebellion, and by specifically calling the proclamation "a fit and necessary war measure" to suppress insurrection. Then he designated those states and parts of states in which the slaves were to be freed (*Alternative 3*), asked them to labor faithfully for wages, and finally invited those of military age to join the armed forces (*Alternative 5*).

The cabinet again reacted favorably, although Seward, Chase, and several others suggested a number of changes. When the document was discussed in greater detail the following day, Chase repeated his advice that Lincoln omit the planned exclusion of parts of states and proposed a closing sentence invoking "the considerate judgment of mankind, and the gracious favor of Almighty God." Bates wanted to leave out all references to the raising of Negro troops, and Seward as well as others offered minor amendments. The president, who had received letters from various quarters asking for special exemptions, rejected Chase's alternative. But he accepted the secretary's felicitous ending, which he strengthened by adding another reference to the constitutionality of his action based on military necessity. Incorporating some of the other editorial improvements, he completed the proclamation. He had made his decision (*Alternative 9:* see Document 15). All that remained was to implement it.

January 1, 1863, was a bright and sunny day. The president rose early to attend to his duties as head of state. The New Year's reception was taxing, as the diplomatic corps and other well-wishers came to shake his hand. But once these formalities were over, he turned to the business of the day. Without special ceremony, he placed his signature on the Emancipation Proclamation. The beginning of the end of human slavery in the United States had come.

Lincoln's final proclamation was not an inspiring document. Notwithstanding Chase's closing sentence, it contained none of the brilliant phrases for which Lincoln was famous. But inspite of its awkwardness, inspite of its imperfections, it became the charter of freedom for millions of human beings (see Document 18). The president had chosen the best possible alternative.

Notes

1. Salmon P. Chase, *Inside Lincoln's Cabinet: The Civil War Diaries of Salmon P. Chase,* ed., David Donald (New York: Longmans, Green, 1954), pp. 105-6.

2. Edgar Cowan to W.H. Seward, August 8, 1862, Robert Todd Lincoln Papers, Library of Congress, Washington, D.C.

3. Roy P. Basler, ed., *The Collected Works of Abraham Lincoln* (New Brunswick, N.J.: Rutgers University Press, 1953), vol. V, p. 343.

4. Ibid., p. 425.

5. Chase, *Diaries,* pp. 49-50.

6. Chase, *Diaries,* p. 151; cf. Document 11.

7. Columbus Crisis, October 29, 1862.

8. Sarah Forbes Hughes, ed., *Letters and Recollections of John Murray Forbes* (Boston, 1899), vol. I, p. 352.

5

Implementation

The promulgation of the Emancipation Proclamation set Lincoln's course for the remainder of the war. How it would be implemented, however, remained an open question. There were those who continued to hope that he might change his mind (*Alternative 8*). At least they believed this option to be open to him. It was also conceivable that slavery might continue to exist in the exempted areas in the South, to say nothing of the border states. But many Republicans were working for different policies. Deeply committed to emancipation throughout the United States, they advocated alternate choices for the administration: either an end to the exemptions; or, as individual states fell to Union forces, state action; or a general law implementing the proclamation (*Alternative 10*). Another possibility was the passage of a constitutional amendment to ensure the permanence of freedom (*Alternative 11*).

The related problems of colonization and compensated emancipation also still had to be considered (*Alternative 6*). Continued worry about anti-Negro prejudice in the North made such policies seem appropriate. Whether they were practical or not, Lincoln necessarily had to take them into account.

The recruiting of Negro troops likewise continued to raise questions. Should military service be confined to free men? Should it provide a road to freedom for remaining slaves? (*Alternative 5*). And should black soldiers and sailors receive the same pay and benefits as their white comrades? In finding solutions for these problems, Lincoln would have to balance carefully existing prejudices and continuing military needs.

As far as the president was concerned, from the outset there was no possibility of revoking the proclamation (*Alternative 9*). His antislavery convictions strongly militated against such a course. As he told Governor Thomas E. Bramlette and ex-Senator Archibald Dixon of Kentucky in the spring of 1864, "I am naturally anti-slavery. If slavery is not wrong, nothing is wrong. I cannot remember when I did not so think, and feel."[1] And although, because of constitutional restrictions, he had not acted upon his convictions when he became president, he nevertheless did so when the life of the nation seemed to require it. Obviously, he was not going to change his mind.

There were also other reasons for Lincoln's refusal to reverse himself. Although the lukewarm foreign reaction to the proclamation was disappointing, he made the most of the diplomatic opportunity it presented. After receiving a letter from the workingmen of Manchester conveying their appreciation for his firmness in upholding emancipation, he carefully composed a detailed reply. Deploring his correspondents' sufferings caused by the cotton shortage, he expressed his admiration for their heroism in behalf of freedom. "I hail this interchange of sentiment . . . ," he concluded, "as an augury that . . . the peace and friendship which now exist between the two nations will be, as it shall be my desire to make them, perpetual" (see Document 14). As Seward pointed out to Senator Browning at a dinner a few days later, it "was not alone the abolition clamor at home" that had induced the president to issue the proclamation. He had been "farther influenced by the wishes of foreign Nations who could not be made to understand our condition."[2] The secretary regretted the edict of freedom, but he believed it could not be changed.

The president made no secret of his determination. Even as he put his name to the proclamation, he told Congressman Schuyler Colfax that the South had had fair warning. Now the promise had to be kept, and he would not recall one word. Senator Browning, still adamantly opposed to the emancipation edict, three weeks later dejectedly admitted in his diary that Judge David Davis had told him the prospects of a change in policy were virtually nil. Davis had tried to induce Lincoln to reverse his course. But the president, in no uncertain terms, repeated what he had earlier told Colfax. The proclamation was a "fixed thing." He intended to adhere to it. The judge concluded that the conservative cause was hopeless.[3]

Even in the face of serious opposition, Lincoln refused to change his mind about emancipation. During the summer of 1863, he received an invitation to address a meeting of Illinois Unionists. Unable to be present in person, he sent a letter making his position clear. "To be plain," he wrote, "you are dissatisfied with me about the negro. Quite likely there is a difference between you and myself upon that subject. I certainly wish that all men could be free, while I suppose you do not."[4] Reaffirming the constitutionality of the proclamation, he insisted that revoking it would not help the cause. On the contrary, some of the commanders in the field considered emancipation and the use of black troops the heaviest blow yet dealt to the rebellion. At any rate, he repeated that the promise of freedom, once made, must be kept.

In spite of his rejection of the most reactionary option open to him, the president still retained considerable freedom of maneuver. Considering the constant pressure from Democratic newspapers, conservative politicians, and the border states, he had to think of viable alternatives of implementation. His own cabinet remained divided between the radical secretaries of the War and Treasury Departments, and their more conservative colleagues. The army called for additional soldiers, while rival Unionist factions in the South presented differing plans of Reconstruction. To keep all these disparate elements united, or at least nominally harmonious, remained one of Lincoln's main tasks.

Reconstruction With Emancipation

The problem soon became acute in the states to be reconstructed. Wartime Reconstruction might well set precedents for postwar action, and the president had to exercise care. He could take the easiest way out and foster the immediate return without conditions of any state willing to resume its allegiance. But would the proclamation apply in such a case? And what of states which were either partially or entirely exempted from the proclamation? Lincoln could also choose another approach and demand an end of slavery as part of the Reconstruction process. In view of the necessity of securing support in Congress for any policy of Reconstruction, even had he not been personally committed to emancipation, he would have reaped benefits from imposing antislavery conditions.

The president chose to insist on emancipation (*Alternative 10*). When, in June, 1863, a committee of conservative Louisiana Unionists asked him to support their plan of restoring the state with its old constitution intact, he replied that he could not comply with their request. Other Louisiana Unionists had informed him that they were in favor of holding a convention to amend the constitution, and he had no intention of denying their wishes. This legalistic phraseology hid the fact that the old constitution sanctioned slavery and was therefore favored by the conservatives. A new charter, or amendments to the old, would presumably entail emancipation. This was the policy of the radicals.

The president soon reaffirmed his commitment to emancipation. When in July 1863 he heard that ex-Senator William K. Sebastian of Arkansas intended to present his credentials to the next session of Congress, Lincoln advised the local military commander that this attempt at Reconstruction might be helped by some positive policy concerning slavery. The Emancipation Proclamation applied to Arkansas. He considered it valid law, bound to be upheld by the courts. "I think I shall not retract or repudiate it," he added. "Those who shall have tasted actual freedom . . . can never be slaves, or quasi slaves again." For the rest, he believed some gradual plan would be best, and if Senator Sebastian would come up "with something of this sort from Arkansas,"[5] the president would take a great interest in the case. Nothing came of this scheme, but Lincoln continued to support efforts to end slavery in the state.

In December 1863, the president decided to formalize and expand his policy of Reconstruction with emancipation. When he published his plan for the restoration of state governments as soon as ten percent of the electorate had taken an oath of allegiance, he specifically required adherence to the Emancipation Proclamation. Freedom for the blacks thus became part of the process of bringing seceded states back into the Union.

Lincoln's decision did not remain mere theory. In Arkansas as well as in Louisiana, new governments were set up in accordance with his plan. In the latter state, especially, he consistently rejected opportunities to collaborate with conservative factions. And although he did not countenance the complete success of the ultraradicals—a policy he rejected because of his efforts to maintain an equilibrium, he more than anybody else was responsible for the inauguration of a free state government in February 1864. As he had written to General N. P. Banks as early as August 1863, "As an anti-slavery man I have a motive to desire emancipation, which pro-slavery men do not have," a sentiment which on December 24 led him to instruct the general "to take the case as you find it, and give us a free-state reorganization of Louisiana."[6]

The Problem of the Border States

In those states exempted from the provisions of the proclamation, Lincoln could have awaited the course of events. He could also have supported conservative proslavery factions in the areas in question. In effect, however, he opted for a different approach (*Alternative 10*). After the twin victories at Gettysburg and Vicksburg, the likelihood of losing the border states diminished, and he proceeded to take strong action in support of emancipation. In Tennessee, he so instructed Governor Andrew Johnson, and by early 1865 a new state constitution outlawed slavery. In Western Virginia, he agreed to the creation of a new state pledged to gradual emancipation, and in Missouri and Maryland, he sought to hurry freedom along without offending the contending factions within each state.

In Missouri, the persistent factionalism of the Unionists created serious trouble. The so-called Claybanks, led by Governor Hamilton Gamble and supported by the powerful Blair family, favored gradual emancipation; the Charcoals, followers of B. Gratz Brown, the editor of the St. Louis *Democrat*, and Charles D. Drake, a skillful politician and excellent debator, demanded instant abolition. The president tried to bring the two parties together. He parried the attacks of the radicals who held him personally responsible for their troubles, but in spite of the ultras' hostility, he confessed to his secretary that the radicals were nearer to him than the other side. "They are absolutely uncorrosive by the virus of secession . . . ," he said. "If one side must be crushed out and the other cherished, there could be no doubt which side we would choose. . . . We would have to side with radicals."[7] In the long run, the Charcoals were successful, and in the beginning of 1865, slavery was abolished by the state convention.

What was true of Missouri was equally true of Maryland. Unionists in the state consisted of conservatives close to the Blair family and radicals led by Henry Winter Davis. Lincoln sought to conciliate both factions, but even though his own postmaster general delivered an ill-timed conservative speech at Rockville in October 1863, the president saw to it that the unconditional Unionists had enough military protection to win the state elections. In the following year, despite the bitter personal hostility of Henry Winter Davis, Lincoln was delighted to see that the radical faction succeeded in calling a state convention and inaugurating emancipation. Although he knew that Davis was his inveterate enemy, he said he did not mind. "If he and the rest can succeed in carrying the State for emancipation," he told the astonished John Hay, "I shall be very willing to lose the electoral vote."[8]

In view of the progress of emancipation in the border states and other exempted areas, Lincoln could well afford to disregard Chase's oft-repeated suggestion that the exemptions of parts of states from the provisions of the proclamation be annulled. No matter how frequently the subject was brought to his attention, the president refused to entertain this alternative of implementing the emancipation policy. The free state constitution of Louisiana and the movement towards abolition in Tennessee would automatically vitiate the exemptions there. Even in Virginia, the restored government of Governor Francis H. Pierpoint was moving towards freedom, a process completed in early 1864. There simply was no further need to recur to the problem. But whenever he was called upon to consider possible peace proposals, Lincoln insisted on emancipation—at least gradual emancipation— as well as submission as a price for reunion.

Colonization, Compensation, and the Black Troops

While actively furthering schemes for freedom in the border states and other exempted areas, the president still sought to assuage public opinion by continuing to investigate the possibilities of colonization (*Alternative 6*). The postmaster general especially kept urging him on, and the Senate asked for information on the subject. He actively supported the experiment at the Ile à Vache, although, after the scheme failed and he had to bring back the remaining colonists, he began to doubt the feasibility of expatriation. Nevertheless, if we are to believe General Butler, as late as early 1865, the president was still willing to contemplate a plan to send black soldiers to Panama. Whether still devoted to colonization or not, he was not prepared to offend public opinion.

Compensated emancipation likewise continued to appeal to the administration (*Alternative 4*). The president mentioned the idea to Senator Browning in January, 1863, and recurred to it in December in his annual message. But at the same time, he repeated his unshakable determination not to "retreat or modify" the Emancipation Proclamation and never to return to slavery anyone already free.[9]

The military question could be solved with comparatively little trouble. As the war used up more and more manpower, resistance to black troops began to lessen. And as time went on, the question of the new recruits' former status was no longer taken so seriously. Congress passed laws freeing all soldiers forever, liberating their families, and finally granting equal pay to black and white troops alike. Lincoln signed all these bills. His cautious approach was so successful that by the end of the war some one hundred eighty thousand black soldiers had fought valiantly for the national cause.

Making Emancipation Permanent: A Constitutional Amendment

The problems of ensuring the permanence of the proclamation, however, remained to be solved (*Alternative 9*). Nothing in the laws or the Constitution could prevent individual states from attempting to annul it, a fact Solicitor Whiting had made quite clear, and the Supreme Court might at any time pronounce it unconstitutional. In addition, both Kentucky and Delaware, border states unaffected by the edict, adamantly refused to put an end to slavery within their limits. Lincoln had to do something. He could either ignore the problem and hope for the best, or he could allow Congress to engraft the reform on the statute books. In either case, however, the constitutional issue of the legality of presidential or congressional interference with the domestic institutions of the states would not have been solved. As a result, Lincoln increasingly turned his attention to a third alternative: emancipation by constitutional amendment (*Alternative 11*).

Amending the Constitution was not an easy process. No change in the country's fundamental law had been made since Thomas Jefferson's administration, and in view of the requirement for a two-thirds vote in both Houses, to say nothing of the necessity of ratification by three-quarters of the states, this record was not surprising. Considering the uncertain position of the rebellious commonwealths, it was not at all clear how any majority could be procured.

But Lincoln decided to press for an emancipation amendment. Convinced that the slavery problem would have to be laid to rest once and for all, certain that he possessed no constitutional power to decree freedom except in his capacity as commander-in-chief of the army and navy in times of actual armed rebellion, he came to the conclusion that an amendment was the answer to his problem. Representative I. N. Arnold of Illinois strongly suggested this solution in December of 1863; resolutions favoring a constitutional change were introduced in Congress, and Lincoln saw that his problem might be solved in this manner. Accordingly, he told Senator Morgan of New York to advocate it in his keynote speech to the 1864 Union Convention; the assembled Republicans incorporated it in the party's platform, and Lincoln, as the nominee, accepted it. He maintained his commitment ever after.

His decision was to be severely tested. In July, 1864, Congress passed the Wade-Davis Bill, its own version of a method for Reconstruction. Among other features, the measure contained a provision abolishing slavery throughout the United States, and the radicals strongly urged the president to sign it. But when the time for action came, he refused. Senator Chandler pointed out to him that the bill abolished slavery; Lincoln replied that he doubted Congress' power to do so. "It is no more than you have done yourself," Chandler objected, only to be told flatly: "I conceive that I may in an emergency do things on military grounds which cannot be done constitutionally by Congress."[10] Accordingly, he pocketed the measure, and the ensuing storm put his own reelection in question. Senator Wade and Representative Davis published a bitter personal attack upon him in the New York *Tribune;* movements to replace him as the party's nominee gained strength, and the military situation appeared so unpromising that he himself lost faith in the likelihood of his reelection. But when the Democrats nominated General McClellan on a peace platform, when the military outlook improved—Atlanta fell on September 2 and in the following weeks General Sheridan swept the valley of Virginia clear of Confederate troops—Lincoln's prospects also began to brighten. In conformity with the radicals' demands, he reorganized his cabinet by dropping the conservative Montgomery Blair. Simultaneously, the ultraradical candidate, General Frémont, who had been nominated in May by a splinter convention, withdrew from the race. In the end, even Wade and Davis rallied to the support of the party. The result was Lincoln's triumphant reelection in November, so that he was once more able to devote time to his scheme for ending slavery by constitutional amendment.

Since the first introduction of the measure in Congress, it had secured the necessary two-thirds in the Senate, where a Select Committee on Slavery and Freedmen had been appointed. But it had run into serious difficulty in the House. When it became evident that the requisite number of votes could not be obtained, the amendment's sponsor, James M. Ashley of Ohio, in order to be able to move for a later reconsideration, changed his vote. He was hopeful of greater strength in the forthcoming winter session of 1864-1865.

When Ashley undertook to make a second attempt to pilot his proposal through the House, he was able to rely on the president's firm support. Lincoln, more than ever convinced that his alternative of solving the question once and for all was correct, actively furthered the measure. He incorporated a strong plea for the amendment in his last annual message, and a process of pressuring wavering Congressmen began. Freely using his patronage, he sought to smoothe Ashley's way. The Ohioan invoked Lincoln's statements condemning slavery, and on January 31, 1865, the House proceeded to ballot. Amid great rejoicing, two-thirds of the members voted "aye." Thus the emancipation amendment passed and was sent to the states for ratification.

Lincoln did not live long enough to witness the final triumph of his policy. On December 18, 1865, the secretary of state announced that three-quarters of the states had ratified the Thirteenth Amendment: slavery ceased to exist in the United States. In arriving at this total, he counted Southern states which had already begun their process of Reconstruction. Whether legal or not, this method was not successfully challenged afterwards. Thus the administration strengthened the Emancipation Proclamation and made it permanent. Lincoln's alternative of announcing freedom for slaves in the insurgent regions and then extending it by constitutional amendment proved its merit. The wartime president, by choosing the appropriate option, truly earned his sobriquet, "The Great Emancipator."

Notes

1. Roy P. Basler, ed., *The Collected Works of Abraham Lincoln* (New Brunswick, N.J.: Rutgers University Press, 1953), vol. VII, p. 281.

2. Theodore C. Pease and J.G. Randall, eds., *The Diary of Orville Hickman Browning* (Springfield, Ill.: Illinois State Historical Society Library, 1927-33), vol. I, p. 618.

3. Ibid., p. 616.

4. Basler, *Collected Works*, vol. VI, p. 407.

5. Ibid., p. 358.

6. Ibid., p. 365; vol. VII, p. 90.

7. Tyler Dennett, ed., *Lincoln and the Civil War in the Diaries and Letters of John Hay* (New York: Dodd, Mead and Co., 1939), p. 135.

8. Ibid., p. 216.

9. Basler, *Collected Works*, vol. VIII, p. 152.

10. Dennett, *Lincoln and the Civil War*, p. 206.

Part two

A. Documents of the Decision

1

Excerpts from a Racist Pamphlet, 1861

Dr. John H. Van Evrie was a New York physician whose views on racial differences and the inferiority of the blacks constitute a good example of the prevailing prejudices with which Lincoln had to deal. The following excerpt is taken from Van Evrie's pamphlet, *Negroes and Negro "Slavery," The First an Inferior Race: The Latter Its Normal Condition* (New York, 1861), which was reprinted from the original 1853 edition with a new introduction to take account of the outbreak of civil war.

Document†

If the "anti-slavery" party was based on truth—if the negro, except in color, was a man like ourselves—if social subordination of this negro was wrong, and the four millions of these people at the South entitled to the same liberty as ourselves—and if the men who made this government designed it to include the inferior races of this continent, and it were really beneficial to equalize and fraternize with these negroes, then, though it may be doubted, if using the common government to bring it about were proper, the *end* in view would be so beneficent, and such a transcendent act of justice to these assumed slaves, that all honest, earnest, and patriotic citizens should promptly sustain the party now striving to accomplish it. But, on the contrary, if this party is based on a stupendous falsehood—if the negro is a different and inferior being, and in his normal condition at the South—and if the men who made this government, designed it for white men alone—then the length and breadth and width and depth of the "anti-slavery" delusion, and the crime of the "anti-slavery" party, which has broken up the Union in a blind crusade after negro freedom, will be fully comprehended by the American people. The whole mighty question, therefore, with all its vast and boundless consequences, hinges on the apparently simple question of *fact*—is the negro, except in color, a man like ourselves, and therefore should be amalgamated in the same system?

†From: John H. Van Evrie, *Negroes and Negro Slavery; the First an Inferior Race: The Second Its Normal Condition* (New York, 1861), pp. vi-vii.

It is absolutely certain that neither the liberty, the rights, nor the interests of one single northern citizen is involved; nothing whatever but a blind, foolish, and monstrous theory which is attempted to be forced on the South. If the people of the two great sections of the country could change places, the vast "anti-slavery" delusion would be exploded in sixty days. But as this is impossible, the next best thing is to explain the actual condition of things in the South to the northern mind. This great work the author has undertaken, not to defend an imaginary slavery, for it needs no defense, but to explain the social order—to demonstrate to the senses, as well as the reason, that the negro is a different and subordinate being, and in his normal condition at the South; and thus to show the enormous and fathomless folly, crime, and impiety wrapped up in the great "anti-slavery" delusion of the day. The former edition of this work was put to press hurriedly, that it contained many errors, but the present one has been carefully revised; and, moreover, the introductory chapter has been rewritten, in order to present a more distinct history of the origin and progress of the great British "anti-slavery" imposture which is now working out its legitimate and designed purpose in the destruction of the American Union.

2

William Whiting, Excerpts from The War Powers of the President

William Whiting, the solicitor of the War Department, provided the legal justification for Lincoln's emancipation policies. Publishing his book, *The War Powers of the President and the Legislative Powers of Congress in Relation to Rebellion, Treason, and Slavery* in 1862, he revised and later reissued it several times with varying titles. The following excerpts are taken from a pamphlet published separately.

Document†

War Power of the President to Emancipate Slaves

The power of the President, as commander-in-chief of the army and navy of the United States, when in actual service, to emancipate the slaves of any belligerent section of the country, if such a measure becomes necessary to save the government from destruction, is not, it is presumed, denied by any respectable authority.

Why the Power Exists. The liberation of slaves is looked upon as a means of embarrassing or weakening the enemy, or of strengthening the military power of our army. If slaves be treated as contraband of war, on the ground that they may be used by their masters to aid in prosecuting war, as employees upon military works, or as laborers furnishing by their industry the means of carrying on hostilities; or if they be treated as, in law, belligerents, following the legal condition of their owners; or if they be deemed loyal subjects having a just claim upon the government to be released from their obligations to give aid and service to disloyal and belligerent masters, in order that they may be free to perform their higher duty of

---

†From: William Whiting, *The War Powers of the President and the Legislative Powers of Congress in Relation to Rebellion, Treason, and Slavery* (Boston, 1862), pp. 66-69.

allegiance and loyalty to the United States; or if they be regarded as subjects of the United States, liable to do military duty; or if they be made citizens of the United States, and soldiers; or if the authority of the masters over their slaves is the means of aiding and comforting the enemy, or of throwing impediments in the way of the government, or depriving it of such aid and assistance in successful prosecution of the war, as slaves would and could afford, if released from the control of the enemy,—or if releasing the slaves would embarrass the enemy, and make it more difficult for them to collect and maintain large armies; in either of these cases, the taking away of these slaves from the "aid and service" of the enemy, and putting them to the aid and service of the United States, is justifiable as an act of war. The ordinary way of depriving the enemy of slaves is by declaring emancipation.

The President is the Sole Judge. "It belongs exclusively to the President to judge when the exigency arises in which he has authority, under the constitution, to call forth the militia, and his decision is conclusive on all other persons."

The constitution confers on the Executive, when in actual war, full belligerent powers. The emancipation of enemy's slaves is a belligerent right. It belongs exclusively to the President, as commander-in-chief, to judge whether he shall exercise his belligerent right to emancipate slaves in those parts of the country which are in rebellion. If exercised in fact, and while the war lasts, his act of emancipation is conclusive and binding forever on all the departments of government, and on all persons whatsoever.

Powers of the President Not Inconsistent With Powers of Congress to Emancipate Slaves. The right of the Executive to strike this blow against his enemy does not deprive Congress of the concurrent right or duty to emancipate enemy's slaves, if in *their judgment* a civil act for that purpose is required by public welfare and common defence, for the purpose of aiding and giving effect to such war measures as the commander-in-chief may adopt.

The military authority of the President is not incompatible with the peace or war powers of Congress; but both coexist, and may be exercised upon the same subject. Thus, when the army captures a regiment of soldiers, the legislature may pass laws relating to the captives. So may Congress destroy slavery by abolishing the laws which sustain it, while the commander of the army may destroy it by capture of slaves, by proclamation, or by other means.

Is Liberation of Enemy's Slaves a Belligerent Right? This is the chief inquiry on this branch of the subject. To answer it we must appeal to the law of nations, and learn whether there is any commanding authority which forbids the use of an engine so powerful and so formidable—an engine which may grind to powder the disloyalty of rebels in arms, while it clears the avenue to freedom for four millions of Americans. It is only the law of nations that can decide this question, because the constitution, having given authority to government to make war, has placed no limit whatever to the war powers. There is, therefore, no legal control over the war powers except the law of nations, and no moral control except the usage of modern civilized belligerents.

3

William H. Seward, "Some Thoughts for the President's Consideration," April 1, 1861

William H. Seward's famous memorandum suggesting Lincoln stress a policy of Union instead of antislavery, and if necessary seek a foreign war to cure domestic ills, was a good example of the type of conservative Republican opinion the president had to consider. He politely rejected the secretary of state's advice about foreign policy and the proposition that Seward direct affairs in general, but he paid heed to the warnings about an antislavery stance (*Alternative 1*).

Document†

Memorandum From Secretary Seward

Some Thoughts for the President's Consideration,
April 1, 1861.

First. We are at the end of a month's administration, and yet without a policy either domestic or foreign.

Second. This, however, is not culpable, and it has even been unavoidable. The presence of the Senate, with the need to meet applications for patronage, have prevented attention to other and more grave matters.

Third. But further delay to adopt and prosecute our policies for both domestic and foreign affairs would not only bring scandal on the administration, but danger upon the country.

Fourth. To do this we must dismiss the applicants for office. But how? I suggest that we make the local appointments forthwith, leaving foreign or general ones for ulterior and occasional action.

Fifth. The policy at home. I am aware that my views are singular, and perhaps not sufficiently explained. My system is built upon this idea as a ruling one, namely that we must

†From: John J. Nicolay and John Hay, eds., *Complete Works of Abraham Lincoln* (New York: Tandy Co., 1905), vol. VI, pp. 234-35.

CHANGE THE QUESTION BEFORE THE PUBLIC FROM ONE UPON SLAVERY, OR ABOUT SLAVERY, for a question upon UNION OR DISUNION: In other words, from what would be regarded as a party question, to one of patriotism or union.

The occupation or evacuation of Fort Sumter, although not in fact a slavery or a party question, is so regarded. Witness the temper manifested by the Republicans in the free States, and even by the Union men in the South.

I would therefore terminate it as a safe means for changing the issue. I deem it fortunate that the last administration created the necessity.

For the rest, I would simultaneously defend and reinforce all the ports in the gulf, and have the navy recalled from foreign stations to be prepared for a blockade. Put the island of Key West under martial law.

This will raise distinctly the question of union or disunion. I would maintain every fort and possession in the South.

Crittenden Resolutions, July 22, 1861, and Remarks, August 2, 1861

Lincoln's difficulties in taking any steps against slavery (*Alternative 1*) can be seen from the following resolution, introduced by Representative John J. Crittenden of Kentucky, and passed on July 22, 1861, by the House with only two negative votes. Two days later, a similar resolution sponsored by Andrew Johnson of Tennessee passed the Senate.

Document†

Resolved, That the present deplorable civil war has been forced upon the country by the disunionists of the southern States now in revolt against the constitutional Government and in arms around the capital; that in this national emergency Congress, banishing all feeling of mere passion or resentment, will recollect only its duty to the whole country; that this war is not waged upon our part in any spirit of oppression, nor for any purpose of conquest or subjugation, nor purpose of overthrowing or interfering with the rights of established institutions of those States: but to defend and maintain the supremacy of the Constitution and to preserve the Union with all the dignity, equality, and rights of the several States unimpaired, that as soon as these objects are accomplished the war ought to cease.

Remarks, August 2, 1861

Representative John J. Crittenden, a distinguished Kentucky Whig, frequently acted as spokesman for the conservative Unionists in the border states. The author of the proposed Crittenden compromise during the secession crisis, he remained loyal but continued to oppose any concessions to antislavery sentiment. The following remarks made on August 2, 1861, during the debate concerning the pending first confiscation bill, illustrate the type of border state thinking the president had to consider in formulating his policies.

†From: *Congressional Globe*, 37th Cong., 1st sess., p. 222.

Document†

Mr. CRITTENDEN. I shall occupy the time of the House but a very few moments. Mr. Speaker, it has been conceded in all time, I believe, that the Federal Government, the Congress of the United States, had no power to legislate upon the subject of slavery within the States. It has been conceded that that was a subject for State legislation only. Does war change the powers of Congress in this respect? It is the absence of all power upon the subject which has prevented your legislation. Absence of all power of legislation in time of peace must be the absence of the same power at all times. The constitutional power of this House does not come and go with a change of circumstances. That is a fixed rule of Congress, permanent, immutable, and made to govern Congress. Now, sir, if you can legislate in regard to slavery in this instance, and if you can, upon certain conditions in time of war, destroy the right of the master to his slave, why cannot you, upon conditions, in time of peace do the same thing? You do it here because the slave is employed to aid the master in the commission of a great crime, that is, the uniting in a civil war. Could you not apply the principle to times of peace, and make the conditions then? If a master uses his slave to aid in the commission of a trespass, or it may be a murder, can you declare that to be a sufficient cause for the liberation of the slave? Why can you not? Because you have no[w] power by your Constitution to touch slavery at all. . . .

You are making a positive law here which the gentleman says may come, and probably will come, before the judiciary for interpretation; and the first question which will arise there is, "is the law consistent with the Constitution?" and that is the question I am discussing now. Whether there is a more latitudinous power given by a state of war, is not the question now. . . .

I am speaking to a particular question, and not answering suppositious causes, I say, in relation to slavery, that Congress never had any power of legislation within the States; and, no longer ago than last session, this body and the Senate, by a majority of two thirds, were willing to make that a provision of the Constitution, when nobody had ever demanded it.

Now, sir, I am not inquiring, nor am I prepared to make an argument, as to powers in a state of war, as to national law, world-wide law. I am interposing a positive statute, and I say if there is no power to do this thing in time of peace, there is no such power at any time. . . .

Now, in reference to treason, which is the crime here. The Constitution defines what it is, and provides for its punishment. It declares that treason against the United States shall consist in levying war against them, and that no person shall be convicted of treason except on the testimony of two witnesses to the same overt act, or on his confession in an open court. It declares that Congress shall have power to declare the punishment of treason; but no attainder of treason shall work corruption of blood, or forfeiture, except during the life of the offender.

†From: *Congressional Globe*, 37th Cong., 1st sess., pp. 411-12.

Now, sir, the crime, declared by this bill, and for which this forfeiture is to take place, is treason—treason by its very definition. It is so considered in this bill. . . . This law undertakes to deprive the owner of slaves of his entire property, and to give complete freedom to the slave. The Constitution says that even on conviction of treason, there shall be no forfeiture of property, of any description beyond the lifetime of the offender.

Now, I ask my friends everywhere if it is not a plain breach of the Constitution that a man shall forfeit his slaves? Whatsoever of property he employs, or permits to be employed in a certain way in aid of treasonable purposes, he shall forfeit absolutely, says this bill; and especially shall he forfeit his slaves forever. That is the language of the bill. The language of the Constitution is that no tittle of his property shall be forfeited for longer than his life. In this, however, else we may differ, there is an apparent unconstitutionality in this bill.

Sir, I will leave the matter with this single remark. This provision of the bill will be considered, and so interpreted abroad, as assuming to Congress a power over slavery. If you can, on conditions, in time of war, abrogate and abolish slavery, it may well be asked, whether you cannot do it in time of peace, on similar conditions of supposed future crime? Are we in a condition now, gentlemen, to hazard this momentous, irritating, agitating, revolutionary question? Is it politic to wage such a war as that? I know that it is forced upon you. Your capital is now threatened, and it is within hearing of the enemy's cannon. You are bound to defend yourselves, and to defend yourselves like men. Shall we send forward to the field a whole catalogue of penal laws to fight this battle with? Arms more impotent were never resorted to. They are beneath the dignity of our great cause. They are outside of the policy which ought to control this Government, and lead us on to success in the war that we are now fighting. If you hold up before your enemies this cloud of penal laws, they will say: "War is better than peace. War is comparative repose." They will say, when they are subdued, or if they choose now to submit, "What next? Have we peace, or is this new army of penal laws then to come into action? Are these penal laws to inflict upon us a long agony of prosecution and forfeiture?"

5

Letters to General John C. Frémont from Lincoln

On August 31, 1861, General John C. Frémont issued an order freeing the insurgents' slaves in Missouri. When Lincoln requested that it be modified, he received a flat refusal and issued his own revocation order. The incident alienated many radicals but strengthened the administration in the border states. It was typical of the president's caution not to let the radicals disturb the situation in the border states.

Document†

Letter to General John C. Frémont

Washington, D.C., September 2, 1861.

My dear Sir: Two points in your proclamation of August 30 give me some anxiety:

First. Should you shoot a man, according to the proclamation, the Confederates would very certainly shoot our best men in their hands in retaliation; and so, man for man, indefinitely. It is, therefore, my order that you allow no man to be shot under the proclamation without first having my approbation or consent.

Second. I think there is great danger that the closing paragraph, in relation to the confiscation of property and the liberating slaves of traitorous owners, will alarm our Southern Union friends and turn them against us; perhaps ruin our rather fair prospect for Kentucky. Allow me, therefore, to ask that you will, as of your own motion, modify that paragraph so as to conform to the first and fourth sections of the act of Congress entitled, "An act to confiscate property used for insurrectionary purposes," approved August 6, 1861, and a copy of which act I herewith send you.

This letter is written in a spirit of caution, and not of censure. I send it by special messenger, in order that it may certainly and speedily reach you.

Yours very truly,
A. LINCOLN.

†From: Nicolay and Hay, *Complete Works*, vol. VI, pp. 350-51, 353.

Order to General Frémont

Washington, September 11, 1861.

Sir: Yours of the 8th, in answer to mine of the 2d instant, is just received. Assuming that you, upon the ground, could better judge of the necessities of your position than I could at this distance, on seeing your proclamation of August 30 I perceived no general objection to it. The particular clause, however, in relation to the confiscation of property and the liberation of slaves appeared to me to be objectionable in its nonconformity to the act of Congress passed the 6th of last August upon the same subjects; and hence I wrote you, expressing my wish that that clause should be modified accordingly. Your answer, just received, expresses the preference on your part that I should make an open order for the modification, which I very cheerfully do. It is therefore ordered that the said clause of said proclamation be so modified, held, and construed as to conform to, and not to transcend, the provisions on the same subject contained in the act of Congress entitled, "An act to confiscate property used for insurrectionary purposes," approved August 6, 1861, and that said act be published at length with this order.

Your obedient servant,
A. LINCOLN.

6

Lincoln's Message to Congress Recommending Compensated Emancipation, March 6, 1862

Lincoln's preferred alternative for the border states was a plan of gradual, compensated emancipation. On March 6, 1862, he sent to Congress his message recommending this solution. Although his proposal was never adopted, he continued to advocate it as the easiest way to end the "peculiar institution" (*Alternative 4*).

Document†

Fellow-citizens of the Senate and House of Representatives: I recommend the adoption of a joint resolution by your honorable bodies, which shall be substantially as follows:

Resolved, That the United States ought to cooperate with any State which may adopt gradual abolishment of slavery, giving to such State pecuniary aid, to be used by such State, in its discretion, to compensate for the inconveniences, public and private, produced by such change of system.

If the proposition contained in the resolution does not meet the approval of Congress and the country, there is the end; but if it does command such approval, I deem it of importance that the States and people immediately interested should be at once distinctly notified of the fact, so that they may begin to consider whether to accept or reject it. The Federal Government would find its highest interest in such a measure, as one of the most efficient means of self-preservation. The leaders of the existing insurrection entertain the hope that this government will ultimately be forced to acknowledge the independence of some part of the disaffected region, and that all the slave States north of such part will then say, "The Union for which we have struggled being already gone, we now choose to go with the Southern section." To deprive them of this hope substantially ends the rebellion; and

†From: Nicolay and Hay, *Complete Works*, vol. VII, pp. 112-15.

the initiation of emancipation completely deprives them of it as to all the States initiating it. The point is not that all the States tolerating slavery would very soon, if at all, initiate emancipation; but that while the offer is equally made to all, the more Northern shall, by such initiation, make it certain to the more Southern that in no event will the former ever join the latter in their proposed confederacy. I say "initiation" because, in my judgment, gradual and not sudden emancipation is better for all. In the mere financial or pecuniary view, any member of Congress, with the census tables and treasury reports before him, can readily see for himself how very soon the current expenditures of this war would purchase, at fair valuation, all the slaves in any named State. Such a proposition on the part of the General Government sets up no claim of a right by Federal authority to interfere with slavery within State limits, referring, as it does, the absolute control of the subject in each case to the State and its people immediately interested. It is proposed as a matter of perfectly free choice with them.

In the annual message, last December, I thought fit to say, "The Union must be preserved, and hence all indispensable means must be employed." I said this not hastily, but deliberately. War has been made, and continues to be, an indispensable means to this end. A practical reacknowledgment of the national authority would render the war unnecessary, and it would at once cease. If, however, resistance continues, the war must also continue; and it is impossible to foresee all the incidents which may attend and all the ruin which may follow it. Such as may seem indispensable, or may obviously promise great efficiency, toward ending the struggle, must and will come.

The proposition now made, though an offer only, I hope it may be esteemed to offense to ask whether the pecuniary consideration tendered would not be of more value to the States and private persons concerned than are the institution and property in it, in the present aspect of affairs?

While it is true that the adoption of the proposed resolution would be merely initiatory and not within itself a practical measure, it is recommended in the hope that it would soon lead to important practical results. In full view of my great responsibility to my God and to my country, I earnestly beg the attention of Congress and the people to the subject.

ABRAHAM LINCOLN.

7

Daniel W. Voorhees, Remarks (March 10, 1862)

The opposition of Northern Democrats to any measure directed against slavery never flagged. It was a constant attitude reflecting the ideas of a large constituency which Lincoln could not disregard entirely (*Alternative 1*). The following excerpt from the *Congressional Globe* shows the virulence with which Daniel W. Voorhees, Democrat of Indiana, attacked the president's plan for compensated emancipation in the border states.

Document†

Mr. VOORHEES. I concur with the gentleman from Ohio as to the propriety of considering this resolution now; and I desire to say that if the people that I have the honor to represent are to pay taxes, in addition to the burdens they at present labor under, for the purpose of buying the slaves of the South, it is best for them to know it at once. I shall vote against any postponement of this question. I, for one, as a member of this House, am fully prepared to act upon it now. If this measure is to be pressed, and to become a part of the policy of the Government, I think it is right and proper that the people should know it soon; that, while groaning under almost untold burdens, while trembling under the weight of taxation upon their shoulders, if this additional burden is to come upon them they may prepare in season their sad and oppressed hearts and almost broken bodies to bear it.

I will say one thing further: that if there is any border slave State man here who is in doubt whether he wants his State to sell its slaves to this Government or not, I represent a people that is in no doubt as to whether they want to become the purchasers. It takes two to make a bargain; and I repudiate, once and forever, for the people whom I represent on this floor, any part or parcel in such a contract. Slavery, wherever it exists under the Constitution, I and my constituents will recognize and respect in its legal rights; the *slave trade*, either domestic or foreign, we are opposed to, and it is no favorite of the Constitution. If *emancipation* means *taxation* on the free States, now lavishing their all for the Union and the Constitution, and ever ready to do so, I am opposed to that cause; and I here take my stand in the name of the people I represent against it.

†From: *Congressional Globe*, 37th Cong., 2d sess., p. 1150.

8

Harrison's Landing Letter, July 7, 1862

Conservative opinion permeated many of the higher echelons of the army (*Alternative 1*). The best known spokesman for antiabolitionist officers was General George Brinton McClellan, who did not hesitate to make his views pointedly known to the commander-in-chief in the famous letter he sent from Harrison's Landing, Virginia, after the unsuccessful conclusion of the Peninsular campaign.

Document†

Headquarters Army of the Potomac,
Camp near Harrison's Landing, Virginia

July 7, 1862.

Mr. President: You have been fully informed that the rebel army is in our front, with the purpose of overwhelming us by attacking our positions, or reducing us by blocking our river communications. I cannot but regard our condition as critical, and I earnestly desire, in view of possible contingencies, to lay before your Excellency, for your private consideration, my general views concerning the existing state of the rebellion, although they do not strictly relate to the situation of this army, or strictly come within the scope of my official duties. These views amount to convictions, and are deeply impressed upon my mind and heart. Our cause must never be abandoned; it is the cause of free institutions and self-government. The Constitution and the Union must be preserved, whatever may be the cost in time, treasure, and blood. If secession is successful, other dissolutions are clearly to be seen in the future. Let neither military disaster, political faction, nor foreign war shake your settled purpose to enforce the equal operation of the laws of the United States upon the people of every State. The time has come when the Government must determine upon a civil and military policy covering the whole ground of our national trouble. The responsibility of determining, declaring, and supporting such civil and military policy, and of directing the whole course of national affairs in regard to the rebellion, must now be assumed and exercised by you, or our cause will be lost. The Constitution gives you power sufficient even for the present terrible exigency.

†From: John J. Nicolay and John Hay, *Abraham Lincoln, A History* (New York, 1890), vol. V, pp. 447-49.

This rebellion has assumed the character of a war. As such it should be regarded, and it should be conducted upon the highest principles known to Christian civilization. It should not be a war looking to the subjugation of the people of any State in any event. It should not be at all a war upon population, but against armed forces and political organizations. Neither confiscation of property, political executions of persons, territorial organization of States, or forcible abolition of slavery should be contemplated for a moment.

In prosecuting the war all private property and unarmed persons should be strictly protected, subject only to the necessities of military operations; all private property taken for military use should be paid or receipted for; pillage and waste should be treated as high crimes, all unnecessary trespass sternly prohibited, and offensive demeanor by the military towards citizens promptly rebuked. Military arrests should not be tolerated, except in places where active hostilities exist; and oaths not required by enactments— constitutionally made—should be neither demanded nor received. Military government should be confined to the preservation of public order and the protection of political rights. Military power should not be allowed to interfere with the relations of servitude, either by supporting or impairing the authority of the master, except for repressing disorder, as in other cases. Slaves, contraband under the act of Congress, seeking military protection, should receive it. The right of the Government to appropriate permanently to its own service claims to slave labor should be asserted, and the right of the owner to compensation therefor should be recognized. This principle might be extended upon grounds of military necessity and security to all the slaves within a particular State, thus working manumission in such State; and in Missouri, perhaps in Western Virginia also, and possibly even in Maryland, the expediency of such a military measure is only a question of time. A system of policy thus constitutional and conservative, and pervaded by the influences of Christianity and freedom, would receive the support of almost all truly loyal men, would deeply impress the rebel masses and all foreign nations, and it might be humbly hoped that it would commend itself to the favor of the Almighty.

Unless the principles governing the further conduct of our struggle shall be made known and approved, the effort to obtain requisite forces will be almost hopeless. A declaration of radical views, especially upon slavery, will rapidly disintegrate our present armies. The policy of the Government must be supported by concentrations of military power. The national forces should not be dispersed in expeditions, posts of occupation, and numerous armies; but should be mainly collected into masses and brought to bear upon the armies of the Confederate States. Those armies thoroughly defeated, the political structure which they support would soon cease to exist.

In carrying out any system of policy which you may form, you will require a commander-in-chief of the army; one who possesses your confidence, understands your views, and who is competent to execute your orders by directing the military forces of the nation to the accomplishment of the objects by you proposed. I do not ask that place for myself. I am willing to serve you in such position as you may assign me, and I will do so as faithfully as ever subordinate served superior.

I may be on the brink of eternity, and as I hope forgiveness from my Maker, I have written this letter with sincerity towards you and from love for my country.

> Very respectfully, your obedient servant,
> G.B. McCLELLAN,
> *Major-General Commanding.*

HIS EXCELLENCY ABRAHAM LINCOLN, President.

9

First Version of the Emancipation Proclamation July 22, 1862

Abraham Lincoln presented the first version of the Emancipation Proclamation to the cabinet on July 22, 1862. Following discussion, it was postponed to a more favorable date. The act cited is the second Confiscation Act, which declared that the property of enemies who did not return to their allegiance within sixty days was subject to seizure (*Alternative 3*).

Document†

Emancipation Proclamation as First Submitted to the Cabinet

July 22, 1862

In pursuance of the sixth section of the act of Congress entitled "An act to suppress insurrection and to punish treason and rebellion, to seize and confiscate property of rebels, and for other purposes," approved July 17, 1862, and which act and the joint resolution explanatory thereof are herewith published, I, Abraham Lincoln, President of the United States, do hereby proclaim to and warn all persons within the contemplation of said sixth section to cease participating in, aiding, countenancing, or abetting the existing rebellion, or any rebellion, against the Government of the United States, and to return to their proper allegiance to the United States, on pain of the forfeitures and seizures as within and by said sixth section provided.

And I hereby make known that it is my purpose, upon the next meeting of Congress, to again recommend the adoption of a practical measure for tendering pecuniary aid to the free choice or rejection of any and all States which may then be recognizing and practically sustaining the authority of the United States, and which may then have voluntarily adopted, or thereafter may voluntarily adopt, gradual abolishment of slavery within such State or States; that the object is to practically restore, thenceforward to be maintained, the constitutional relation between the General Government and each and all the States wherein that relation is now suspended or disturbed; and that for this object the war, as it has been, will be prosecuted. And as a fit and necessary military measure for effecting this object, I, as commander-

†From: Nicolay and Hay, *Complete Works*, vol. VII, pp. 289-90.

in-chief of the army and navy of the United States, do order and declare that on the first day of January, in the year of our Lord one thousand eight hundred and sixty-three, all persons held as slaves within any State or States wherein the constitutional authority of the United States shall not then be practically recognized, submitted to, and maintained, shall then, thenceforward, and forever be free.

10

Francis B. Carpenter, Lincoln's Account of the Emancipation Proclamation, (1864-65)

Commissioned to paint a picture of the promulgation of the Emancipation Proclamation, the artist Francis B. Carpenter stayed in the White House for a few months in 1864 and 1865. When he recounted his experiences shortly afterwards, he included the earliest version of the origin of the document attributed to Lincoln himself (*Alternative 3*).

Document†

The appointed hour found me at the well-remembered door of the official chamber,—that door watched daily, with so many conflicting emotions of hope and fear, by the anxious throng regularly gathered there. The President had preceded me, and was already deep in Acts of Congress, with which the writing-desk was strewed, awaiting his signature. He received me pleasantly, giving me a seat near his own arm-chair; and after having read Mr. Lovejoy's note, he took off his spectacles, and said, "Well, Mr. C——, we will turn you in loose here, and try to give you a good chance to work out your idea." Then, without paying much attention to the enthusiastic expression of my ambitious desire and purpose, he proceeded to give me a detailed account of the history and issue of the great proclamation.

"It had got to be," said he, "midsummer, 1862. Things had gone on from bad to worse, until I felt that we had reached the end of our rope on the plan of operations we had been pursuing; that we had about played our last card, and must change our tactics, or lose the game! I now determined upon the adoption of the emancipation policy; and, without consultation with, or the knowledge of the Cabinet, I prepared the original draft of the proclamation, and, after much anxious thought, called a Cabinet meeting upon the subject.

†From: Francis B. Carpenter, *Six Months at the White House with Abraham Lincoln: The Story of a Picture* (New York, 1867), pp. 20-23.

This was the last of July, or the first part of the month of August, 1862."
(The exact date he did not remember.) "This Cabinet meeting took place, I
think, upon a Saturday. All were present, excepting Mr. Blair, the
Postmaster-General, who was absent at the opening of the discussion, but
came in subsequently. I said to the Cabinet that I had resolved upon this step,
and had not called them together to ask their advice, but to lay the
subject-matter of a proclamation before them; suggestions as to which would
be in order, after they had heard it read. Mr. Lovejoy," said he, "was in error
when he informed you that it excited no comment, excepting on the part of
Secretary Seward. Various suggestions were offered. Secretary Chase wished
the language stronger in reference to the arming of the blacks. Mr. Blair, after
he came in, deprecated the policy, on the ground that it would cost the
Administration the fall elections. Nothing, however, was offered that I had
not already fully anticipated and settled in my own mind, until Secretary
Seward spoke. He said in substance: 'Mr. President, I approve of the
proclamation, but I question the expediency of its issue at this juncture. The
depression of the public mind, consequent upon our repeated reverses, is so
great that I fear the effect of so important a step. It may be viewed as the last
measure of an exhausted government, a cry for help; the government
stretching forth its hands to Ethiopia, instead of Ethiopia stretching forth her
hands to the government.' His idea," said the President, "was that it would be
considered our last *shriek*, on the retreat." (This was his *precise* expression.)
" 'Now,' continued Mr. Seward, 'while I approve the measure, I suggest, sir,
that you postpone its issue, until you can give it to the country supported by
military success, instead of issuing it, as would be the case now, upon the
greatest disasters of the war!' " Mr. Lincoln continued: "The wisdom of the
view of the Secretary of State struck me with very great force. It was an
aspect of the case that, in all my thought upon the subject, I had entirely
overlooked. The result was that I put the draft of the proclamation aside, as
you do your sketch for a picture, waiting for a victory. From time to time I
added or changed a line, touching it up here and there, anxiously watching
the progress of events. Well, the next news we had was of Pope's disaster, at
Bull Run. Things looked darker than ever. Finally, came the week of the
battle of Antietam. I determined to wait no longer. The news came, I think,
on Wednesday, that the advantage was on our side. I was then staying at the
Soldiers' Home, (three miles out of Washington.) Here I finished writing the
second draft of the preliminary proclamation; came up on Saturday; called
the Cabinet together to hear it, and it was published the following Monday."
    At the final meeting of September 20th, another interesting incident
occurred in connection with Secretary Seward. The President had written the
important part of the proclamation in these words:—
    "That, on the first day of January, in the year of our Lord one thousand
eight hundred and sixty-three, all persons held as slaves within any State or
designated part of a State, the people whereof shall then be in rebellion
against the United States, shall be then, thenceforward, and forever FREE;
and the Executive Government of the United States, including the military

and naval authority thereof, will *recognize* the freedom of such persons, and will do no act or acts to repress such persons, or any of them, in any efforts they may make for their actual freedom." "When I finished reading this paragraph," resumed Mr. Lincoln, "Mr. Seward stopped me, and said, 'I think, Mr. President, that you should insert after the word *"recognize,"* in that sentence, the words *"and maintain."* ' I replied that I had already fully considered the import of that expression in this connection, but I had not introduced it, because it was not my way to promise what I was not entirely *sure* that I could perform, and I was not prepared to say that I thought we were exactly able to 'maintain' this."

"But," said he, "Seward insisted that we ought to take this ground; and the words finally went in!"

"It is a somewhat remarkable fact," he subsequently remarked, "that there were just one hundred days between the dates of the two proclamations issued upon the 22d of September and the 1st of January. I had not made the calculation at the time."

11

Horace Greeley, "The Prayer of Twenty Millions," August 19, 1862, and Lincoln's Reply, August 22, 1862

Horace Greeley's open letter in the New York *Tribune*, dated August 19, 1862, and entitled "The Prayer of Twenty Millions," represents a good example of the antislavery pressure to which the president had to respond (*Alternative 2*). Although he had already decided to issue an emancipation proclamation, his resolve was not publicly known, and he replied in his characteristically cautious way. In his last sentence, however, he unmistakably stated his private views concerning the evils of slavery.

Document†

The Prayer of Twenty Millions.

To Abraham Lincoln, President of the United States:

Dear Sir: I do not intrude to tell you—for you must know already—that a great proportion of those who triumphed in your election, and of all who desire the unqualified suppression of the rebellion now desolating our country, are sorely disappointed and deeply pained by the policy you seem to be pursuing with regard to the slaves of rebels. I write only to set succinctly and unmistakably before you what we require, what we think we have a right to expect, and of what we complain.

I. We require of you, as the first servant of the Republic, charged especially and preeminently with this duty, that you EXECUTE THE LAWS. Most emphatically do we demand that such laws as have been recently enacted, which therefore may fairly be presumed to embody the *present* will

†From: Frank Moore, ed., *The Rebellion Record* (New York, 1862-68), Sup., vol. I, part II, pp. 480-83.

and to be dictated by the *present* needs of the Republic, and which, after due consideration, have received your personal sanction, shall by you be carried into full effect, and that you publicly and decisively instruct your subordinates that such laws exist, that they are binding on all functionaries and citizens, and that they are to be obeyed to the letter.

II. We think you are strangely and disastrously remiss in the discharge of your official and imperative duty with regard to the emancipation provisions of the new Confiscation Act. Those provisions were designed to fight Slavery with Liberty. They prescribe that men loyal to the Union, and willing to shed their blood in her behalf, shall no longer be held, with the nation's consent, in bondage to persistent, malignant traitors, who for twenty years have been plotting and for sixteen months have been fighting to divide and destroy our country. Why these traitors should be treated with tenderness by you, to the prejudice of the dearest rights of loyal men, we cannot conceive.

III. We think you are unduly influenced by the councils, the representations, the menaces, of certain fossil politicians hailing from the Border Slave States. Knowing well that the heartily, unconditionally loyal portion of the white citizens of those States do not expect nor desire that Slavery shall be upheld to the prejudice of the Union—(for the truth of which we appeal not only to every Republican residing in those States, but to such eminent loyalists as H. Winter Davis, Parson Brownlow, the Union Central Committee of Baltimore, and to *The Nashville Union*)—we ask you to consider that Slavery is everywhere the inciting cause and sustaining base of treason: the most slaveholding sections of Maryland and Delaware being this day, though under the Union flag, in full sympathy with the rebellion, while the free labor portions of Tennessee and of Texas, though writhing under the bloody heel of treason, are unconquerably loyal to the Union. So emphatically is this the case, that a most intelligent Union banker of Baltimore recently avowed his confident belief that a majority of the present Legislature of Maryland, though elected as and still professing to be Unionists, are at heart desirous of the triumph of the Jeff Davis conspiracy; and when asked how they could be won back to loyalty, replied—"Only by the complete Abolition of Slavery." It seems to us the most obvious truth, that whatever strengthens or fortifies Slavery in the Border States strengthens also treason, and drives home the wedge intended to divide the Union. Had you, from the first, refused to recognize in those States, as here, any other than unconditional loyalty—that which stands for the Union, whatever may become of Slavery—those States would have been, and would be, far more helpful and less troublesome to the defenders of the Union than they have been, or now are.

IV. We think timid counsels in such a crisis calculated to prove perilous, and probably disastrous. It is the duty of a Government so wantonly, wickedly assailed by rebellion as ours has been, to oppose force to force in a defiant, dauntless spirit. It cannot afford to temporize with traitors, nor with semi-traitors. It must not bribe them to behave themselves, nor make them fair promises in the hope of disarming their causeless hostility. Representing a brave and highspirited people, it can afford to forfeit any thing else better than its own self-respect, or their admiring confidence. For our Government even to seek, after war has been made on it, to dispel the affected apprehensions of armed traitors that their cherished privileges may be assailed by it, is to invite insult and encourage hopes of its own downfall. The rush to arms of Ohio, Indiana, Illinois, is the true answer at once to the rebel raids of John Morgan and the traitorous sophistries of Beriah Magoffin.

V. We complain that the Union cause has suffered, and is now suffering immensely, from mistaken deference to rebel Slavery. Had you, sir, in your Inaugural Address, unmistakably given notice that, in case the rebellion already commenced, were persisted in, and your efforts to preserve the Union and enforce the laws should be resisted by armed force, *you would recognize no loyal person as rightfully held in Slavery by a traitor*, we believe the rebellion would therein have received a staggering if not fatal blow. At that moment, according to the returns of the most recent elections, the Unionists were a large majority of the voters of the slave States. But they were composed in good part of the aged, the feeble, the wealthy, the timid—the young, the reckless, the aspiring, the adventurous, had already been largely lured by the gamblers and negro-traders, the politicians by trade and the conspirators by instinct, into the toils of treason. Had you then proclaimed that rebellion would strike the shackles from the slaves of every traitor, the wealthy and the cautious would have been supplied with a powerful inducement to remain loyal. As it was, every coward in the South soon became a traitor from fear; for loyalty was perilous, while treason seemed comparatively safe. Hence the boasted unanimity of the South—a unanimity based on rebel terrorism and the fact that immunity and safety were found on that side, danger and probable death on ours. The rebels, from the first, have been eager to confiscate, imprison, scourge, and kill; we have fought wolves with the devices of sheep. The result is just what might have been expected. Tens of thousands are fighting in the rebel ranks to-day, whose original bias and natural leanings would have led them into ours.

VI. We complain that the Confiscation Act which you approved is habitually disregarded by your Generals, and that no word of rebuke for them from you has yet reached the public ear. Fremont's Proclamation and Hunter's Order favoring Emancipation were promptly annulled by you; while Halleck's Number Three, forbidding fugitives from slavery to rebels to come within his lines—an order as unmilitary as inhuman, and which received the hearty approbation of every traitor in America—with scores of like tendency, have never provoked even your remonstrance. We complain that the officers of your armies have habitually repelled rather than invited the approach of slaves who would have gladly taken the risks of escaping from their rebel masters to our camps, bringing intelligence often of inestimable value to the Union cause. We complain that those who *have* thus escaped to us, avowing a willingness to do for us whatever might be required, have been brutally and madly repulsed, and often surrendered to be scourged, maimed, and tortured by the ruffian traitors, who pretend to own them. We complain that a large proportion of our regular army officers, with many of the volunteers, evince far more solicitude to uphold Slavery than to put down the rebellion. And finally, we complain that you, Mr. President, elected as a Republican, knowing well what an abomination Slavery is, and how emphatically it is the core and essence of this atrocious rebellion, seem never to interfere with these atrocities, and never give a direction to your military subordinates, which does not appear to have been conceived in the interest of Slavery rather than of Freedom.

VII. Let me call your attention to the recent tragedy in New-Orleans, whereof the facts are obtained entirely through pro-slavery channels. A considerable body of resolute, able-bodied men, held in slavery by two rebel sugar-planters in defiance of the Confiscation Act which you have approved, left plantations thirty miles distant and made their way to the great mart of the South-West, which they knew to be in the undisputed possession of the Union forces. They made their way safely and quitely through thirty miles of rebel territory, expecting to find freedom under the protection of our flag. Whether they had or had not heard of the passage of the Confiscation Act, they reasoned logically that we could not kill them for deserting the service of their lifelong oppressors, who had through treason become our implacable enemies. They came to us for liberty and protection, for which they were willing to render their best service; they met with hostility, captivity, and murder. The barking of the base curs of slavery in this quarter deceives no one—not even themselves. They say, indeed, that the negroes had no right to appear in New-Orleans armed, (with their implements of daily labor in the cane-field;) but no one doubts that they would gladly have laid these down if assured that they should be free. They were set upon and maimed, captured and killed, because they sought the benefit of that act of Congress which they may not specifically have heard of, but which was none the less the law of the land—which they had a clear *right* to the benefit of—which it was *somebody's* duty to publish far and wide, in order that so many as possible should be impelled to desist from serving rebels and the rebellion, and come over to the side of the Union. They sought their liberty in strict accordance with the law of the land—they were butchered or reenslaved for so doing by the help of Union soldiers enlisted to fight against slaveholding treason. It was *somebody's* fault that they were so murdered—if others shall hereafter suffer in like manner, in default of explicit and public direction to your generals that they are to recognize and obey the Confiscation Act, the world will lay the blame on *you.* Whether you will choose to hear it through future history and at the bar of God, I will not judge. I can only hope.

VIII. On the face of this wide earth, Mr. President, there is not one disinterested, determined, intelligent champion of the Union cause who does not feel that all attempts to put down the rebellion and at the same time uphold its inciting cause are preposterous and futile—that the rebellion, if crushed out to-morrow, would be renewed within a year if Slavery were left in full vigor—that army officers who remain to this day devoted to Slavery can at best be half-way loyal to the Union and that every hour of deference to Slavery is an hour of added and deepened peril to the Union. I appeal to the testimony of your Embassadors in Europe. It is freely at your service, not at mine. Ask them to tell you candidly whether the seeming subserviency of your policy to the slaveholding, slavery-upholding interest, is not the perplexity, the despair of statesmen of all parties, and be admonished by the general answer!

IX. I close as I began with the statement that what an immense majority of the loyal millions of your countrymen require of you is a frank, declared, unqualified, ungrudging execution of the laws of the land, more especially of the Confiscation Act. That act gives freedom to the slaves of rebels coming within our lines, or whom those lines may at any time inclose—we ask you to render it due obedience by publicly requiring all your subordinates to recognize and obey it. The rebels are everywhere using the late anti-negro riots in the North, as they have long used your officers' treatment of negroes in the South, to convince the slaves that they have nothing to hope from a Union success—that we mean in that case to sell them into a bitter bondage to defray the cost of the war. Let them impress this as a truth on the great mass of their ignorant and credulous bondmen, and the Union will never be restored—never. We cannot conquer ten millions of people united in solid phalanx against us, powerfully aided by Northern sympathizers and European allies. We must have scouts, guides, spies, cooks, teamsters, diggers, and choppers from the blacks of the South, whether we allow them to fight for us or not, or we shall be baffled and repelled. As one of the millions who would gladly have avoided this struggle at any sacrifice but that of principle and honor, but who now feel that the triumph of the Union is indispensable not only to the existence of our country but to the well-being of mankind, I entreat you to render a hearty and unequivocal obedience to the law of the land.

Yours,
HORACE GREELEY.

New-York, August 19, 1862.

President Lincoln's Letter.
Executive Mansion, Washington

August 22, 1862

Hon. Horace Greeley:

Dear Sir: I have just read yours of the nineteenth, addressed to myself through the New York *Tribune.* If there be in it any statements or assumptions of fact which I may know to be erroneous, I do not now and here controvert them. If there be in it any inferences which I may believe to be falsely drawn, I do not now and here argue against them. If there be perceptible in it an impatient and dictatorial tone, I waive it in deference to an old friend, whose heart I have always supposed to be right.

As to the policy I "seem to be pursuing," as you say, I have not meant to leave any one in doubt.

I would save the Union. I would save it the shortest way under the Constitution. The sooner the National authority can be restored, the nearer the Union will be "the Union as it was." If there be those who would not save the Union unless they could at the same time *save* Slavery, I do not agree with them. If there be those who would not save the Union unless they could at the same time *destroy* Slavery, I do not agree with them. My paramount object in this struggle *is* to save the Union, and is *not* either to save or destroy Slavery. If I could save the Union without freeing *any* slave, I would do it; and if I could save it by freeing *all* the slaves, I would do it; and if I could do it by freeing some and leaving others alone, I would also do that. What I do about Slavery and the colored race, I do because I believe it helps o save this Union; and what I forbear, I forbear because I do *not* believe it would help to save the Union. I shall do *less* whenever I shall believe what I am doing hurts the cause, and I shall do *more* whenever I shall believe doing more will help the cause. I shall try to correct errors when shown to be errors; and I shall adopt new views so fast as they shall appear to be true views. I have here stated my purpose according to my view of *official* duty, and I intend no modification of my oft-expressed *personal* wish that all men, everywhere, could be free.

Yours,
A. LINCOLN.

12

Abraham Lincoln, Preliminary Emancipation Proclamation, September 22, 1862

The Preliminary Emancipation Proclamation, largely Lincoln's own composition, was the first public announcement of the policy which led to the promulgation of the final document one hundred days later (*Alternatives 3 and 6*). For Lincoln's own account, see Document 10, above.

Document†

By the President of the United States of America. I, Abraham Lincoln, President of the United States of America, and Commander-in-Chief of the Army and Navy thereof, do hereby proclaim and declare that hereafter as heretofore the war will be prosecuted for the object of practically restoring the constitutional relation between the United States and the people thereof in those States in which that relation is, or may be, suspended or disturbed; that it is my purpose upon the next meeting of Congress to again recommend the adoption of a practical measure tendering pecuniary aid to the free acceptance or rejection of all the slave States, so-called, the people whereof may not then be in rebellion against the United States, and which States may then have voluntarily adopted, or thereafter may voluntarily adopt, the immediate or gradual abolishment of slavery within their respective limits, and that the effort to colonize persons of African descent, with their consent, upon the continent or elsewhere, with the previously obtained consent of the government existing there, will be continued; that on the first day of January, in the year of our Lord one thousand eight hundred and sixty-three, all persons held as slaves within any State, or any designated part of a State, the people whereof shall then be in rebellion against the United States shall be then, thenceforward and forever, free, and the executive government of the United States, including the military and naval authority thereof, will

†From: Frank Moore, *Rebellion Record,* vol. V, part III, pp. 479-80.

recognize and maintain the freedom of such persons, and will do no act or acts to repress such persons, or any of them, in any efforts they may make for their actual freedom, that the Executive will, on the first day of January aforesaid, by proclamation, designate the States and parts of States, if any, in which the people thereof respectively shall then be in rebellion against the United States; and the fact that any State, or the people thereof, shall on that day be in good faith represented in the Congress of the United States by members chosen thereto, at elections wherein a majority of the qualified voters of such State shall have participated, shall, in the absence of strong countervailing testimony, be deemed conclusive evidence that such State and the people thereof have not been in rebellion against the United States.

That attention is hereby called to an act of Congress entitled, "An act to make an additional article of war," approved March 13, 1862, and which act is in the words and figure following:

"Be it enacted by the Senate and House of Representatives of the United States of America, in Congress assembled, That hereafter the following shall be promulgated as an additional article of war for the government of the army of the United States, and shall be observed and obeyed as such.

"Article—. All officers or persons of the military or naval service of the United States are prohibited from employing any of the forces under their respective commands for the purpose of returning fugitives from service or labor who may have escaped from any persons to whom such service or labor is claimed to be due, and any officer who shall be found guilty by a court-martial of violating this article, shall be dismissed from the service.

"Sec. 2. And be it further enacted, That this act shall take effect from and after its passage."

Also to the ninth and tenth sections of an act entitled, "An act to suppress insurrection, to punish treason and rebellion, to seize and confiscate property of rebels, and for other purposes," approved July 17, 1862, and which sections are in the words and figures following:

"Sec. 9. And be it further enacted, That all slaves of persons who shall hereafter be engaged in rebellion against the government of the United States, or who shall in any way give aid or comfort thereto, escaping from such persons and taking refuge within the lines of the army; and all slaves captured from such persons or deserted by them, and coming under the control of the government of the United States, and all slaves of such persons found on (or being within) any place occupied by rebel forces and afterwards occupied by the forces of the United States, shall be deemed captives of war, and shall be forever free of their servitude and not again held as slaves.

"Sec. 10. And be it further enacted, That no slave escaping into any State, Territory, or the District of Columbia, from any of the States, shall be delivered up, or in any way impeded or hindered of his liberty, except for crime, or some offence against the laws, unless the person claiming said fugitive shall first make oath that the person to whom the labor or service of such fugitive is alleged to be due, is his lawful owner, and has not been in arms against the United States in the present rebellion, nor in any way given aid and comfort thereto; and no person engaged in the military or naval service of the United States shall, under any pretence whatever, assume to decide on the validity of the claim of any person to the service or labor of any other person, or surrender up any such person to the claimant, on pain of being dismissed from the service."

And I do hereby enjoin upon, and order all persons engaged in the military and naval service of the United States to observe, obey and enforce within their respective spheres of service the act and sections above recited.

And the Executive will in due time recommend that all citizens of the United States who shall have remained loyal thereto throughout the rebellion shall (upon the restoration of the constitutional relation between the United States and their respective States and people if the relation shall have been suspended or disturbed) be compensated for all losses by acts of the United States, including the loss of slaves.

In witness whereof, I have hereunto set my hand and caused the seal of the United States to be affixed.

Done at the city of Washington this twenty-second day of September, in the year of our Lord one thousand eight hundred and sixty-two, and of the Independence of the United States the eighty-seventh.

By the President:
ABRAHAM LINCOLN.
WM. H. SEWARD,
Secretary of State.

13

Lincoln's Message to Congress, December 1, 1862

In his second annual message to Congress, Lincoln recurred to his favorite scheme of gradual, compensated emancipation in the slave states (*Alternative 4*). Although the proposal was eventually superseded by the Emancipation Proclamation and the Thirteenth Amendment, its reiteration during the period intervening between the preliminary and final proclamations facilitated Lincoln's policies vis-à-vis the conservatives, especially as he also humored them by once more proposing colonization (*Alternative 6*).

Document†

Our strife pertains to ourselves—to the passing generations of men; and it can without convulsion be hushed forever with the passing of one generation.

In this view I recommend the adoption of the following resolution and articles amendatory to the Constitution of the United States:

"Resolved by the Senate and House of Representatives of the United States of America in Congress assembled (two-thirds of both houses concurring), That the following articles be proposed to the legislatures (or conventions) of the several States as amendments to the Constitution of the United States, all or any of which articles when ratified by three fourths of the said legislatures (or conventions) to be valid as part or parts of the said Constitution, viz.:

"Article—.

"Every state wherein slavery now exists which shall abolish the same therein at any time or times before the first day of January in the year of our Lord one thousand and nine hundred, shall receive compensation from the United States as follows, to wit:

"The President of the United States shall deliver to every such State bonds of the United States, bearing interest at the rate of   per cent. per annum, to an amount equal to the aggregate sum of   for each slave shown to have been therein by the eighth census of the United States, said bonds to be delivered to such State by instalments, or in one

†From: Nicolay and Hay, *Complete Works*, vol. VIII, pp. 116-21.

parcel at the completion of the abolishment, accordingly as the same shall have been gradual or at one time within such State; and interest shall begin to run upon any such bond only from the proper time of its delivery as aforesaid. Any State having received bonds as aforesaid, and afterward reintroducing or tolerating slavery therein, shall refund to the United States the bonds so perceived, or the value thereof, and all interest paid thereon.

"Article—.

"All slaves who shall have enjoyed actual freedom by the chances of the war at any time before the end of the rebellion, shall be forever free; but all owners of such who shall not have been disloyal shall be compensated for them at the same rates as are provided for States adopting abolishment of slavery, but in such way that no slave shall be twice accounted for.

"Article—.

"Congress may appropriate money and otherwise provide for colonizing free colored persons, with their own consent, at any place or places without the United States."

I beg indulgence to discuss these proposed articles at some length. Without slavery the rebellion could never have existed; without slavery it could not continue.

Among the friends of the Union there is great diversity of sentiment and of policy in regard to slavery and the African race amongst us. Some would perpetuate slavery; some would abolish it suddenly and without compensation; some would abolish it gradually, and with compensation; some would remove the freed people from us, and some would retain them with us; and there are yet other minor diversities. Because of these diversities we waste much strength in struggles among ourselves. By mutual concession we should harmonize and act together. This would be compromise; but it would be compromise among the friends, and not with the enemies of the Union. These articles are intended to embody a plan of such mutual concessions. If the plan shall be adopted, it is assumed that emancipation will follow at least in several of the States.

As to the first article, the main points are: first, the emancipation; secondly, the length of time for consummating it—thirty-seven years; and, thirdly, the compensation.

The emancipation will be unsatisfactory to the advocates of perpetual slavery; but the length of time should greatly mitigate their dissatisfaction. The time spares both races from the evils of sudden derangement—in fact, from the necessity of any derangement; while most of those whose habitual course of thought will be disturbed by the measure will have passed away before its consummation. They will never see it. Another class will hail the prospect of emancipation, but will deprecate the length of time. They will feel that it gives too little to the now living slaves. But it really gives them much. It saves them from the vagrant destitution which must largely attend immediate emancipation in localities where their numbers are very great; and it gives the inspiring assurance that their posterity shall be free forever. The plan leaves to each State choosing to act under it to abolish slavery now, or at the end of the century, or at any intermediate time, or by degrees extending over the whole or any part of the period; and it obliges no two States to proceed alike. It also provides for compensation, and generally the mode of making it. This, it would seem, must further mitigate the dissatisfaction of those who favor perpetual slavery, and especially of those who are to receive the compensation. Doubtless some of those who are to pay, and not to receive, will object. Yet the measure is both just and economical. In a certain sense the liberation of slaves is the destruction of property—property acquired by descent or by purchase, the same as any other property. It is no less true for having been often said, that the people of the South are not more responsible for the original introduction of this property than are the people of the North; and when it is remembered how unhesitatingly we all use cotton and sugar and share the profits of dealing in them, it may not be quite safe to say that the South has been more responsible than the North for its continuance. If, then, for a common object this property is to be sacrificed, is it not just that it be done at a common charge?

And if, with less money, or money more easily paid, we can preserve the benefits of the Union by this means than we can by the war alone, is it not also economical to do it? Let us consider it then. Let us ascertain the sum we have expended in the war since compensated emancipation was proposed last March, and consider whether, if that measure had been promptly accepted by even some of the slave States, the same sum would not have done more to close the war than has been otherwise done. If so, the measure would save money, and in that view would be a prudent and economical measure. Certainly it is not so easy to pay something as it is to pay nothing; but it is easier to pay a large sum than it is to pay a larger one. And it is easier to pay any sum when we are able, than it is to pay it before we are able. The war requires large sums, and requires them at once. The aggregate sum necessary for compensated emancipation of course would be large. But it would require no ready cash, nor the bonds even, any faster than the emancipation progresses. This might not, and probably would not, close before the end of the thirty-seven years. At that time we shall probably have 100,000,000 of people to share the burden, instead of 31,000,000 as now. And not only so, but the increase of our population may be expected to continue for a long time after that period as rapidly as before, because our territory will not have become full. I do not state this inconsiderately. At the same ratio of increase which we have maintained, on an average, from our first national census of 1790 until that of 1860, we should in 1900 have a population of 103,208,415. And why may we not continue that ratio far beyond that period? Our abundant room—our broad national homestead—is our ample resource. Were our territory as limited as are the British Isles, very certainly our population could not expand as stated. Instead of receiving the foreign-born as now, we should be compelled to send part of the native-born away. But such is not our condition.

14

Lincoln's Correspondence with the Workingmen of Manchester, December 31, 1862, and January 19, 1863

Lincoln's sensitivity to foreign opinion was one of the factors inducing him to issue the Emancipation Proclamation (*Alternative 9*). His correspondence with a meeting of workingmen, held at Manchester, England, on December 31, 1862, is a good indication of his attempts to reap maximum diplomatic benefits from his antislavery policy.

Document†

To Abraham Lincoln, President of the United States: As citizens of Manchester, assembled at the Free-Trade Hall, we beg to express our fraternal sentiments toward you and your country. We rejoice in your greatness as an outgrowth of England, whose blood and language you share, whose orderly and legal freedom you have applied to new circumstances, over a region immeasurably greater than our own. We honor your Free States, as a singularly happy abode for the working millions where industry is honored. One thing alone has, in the past, lessened our sympathy with your country and our confidence in it—we mean the ascendency of politicians who not merely maintained negro slavery, but desired to extend and root it more firmly. Since we have discerned, however, that the victory of the free North, in the war which has so sorely distressed us as well as afflicted you, will strike off the fetters of the slave, you have attracted our warm and earnest sympathy. We joyfully honor you, as the President, and the Congress with you, for many decisive steps toward practically exemplifying your belief in

†From: Frank Moore, *Rebellion Record*, vol. VI, part II, pp. 344-45, 420-21.

the words of your great founders: "All men are created free and equal." You have procured the liberation of the slaves in the district around Washington, and thereby made the centre of your Federation visibly free. You have enforced the laws against the slave-trade, and kept up your fleet against it, even while every ship was wanted for service in your terrible war. You have nobly decided to receive embassadors from the negro republics of Hayti and Liberia, thus forever renouncing that unworthy prejudice which refuses the rights of humanity to men and women on account of their color. In order more effectually to stop the slave-trade, you have made with our Queen a treaty, which your Senate has ratified, for the right of mutual search. Your Congress has decreed freedom as the law forever in the vast unoccupied or half unsettled Territories which are directly subject to its legislative power. It has offered pecuniary aid to all States which will enact emancipation locally, and has forbidden your Generals to restore fugitive slaves who seek their protection. You have entreated the slave-masters to accept these moderate offers; and after long and patient waiting, you, as Commander-in-Chief of the Army, have appointed to-morrow, the first of January, 1863, as the day of unconditional freedom for the slaves of the rebel States. Heartily do we congratulate you and your country on this humane and righteous course. We assume that you cannot now stop short of a complete uprooting of slavery. It would not become us to dictate any details, but there are broad principles of humanity which must guide you. If complete emancipation in some States be deferred, though only to a predetermined day, still in the interval, human beings should not be counted chattels. Women must have the rights of chastity and maternity, men the rights of husbands, masters the liberty of manumission. Justice demands for the black, no less than for the white, the protection of law—that his voice be heard in your courts. Nor must any such abomination be tolerated as slave-breeding States, and a slave market—if you are to earn the high reward of all your sacrifices, in the approval of the universal brotherhood and of the Divine Father. It is for your free country to decide whether any thing but immediate and total emancipation can secure the most indispensable rights of humanity against the inveterate wickedness of local laws and local executives. We implore you, for your own honor and welfare, not to faint in your providential mission. While your enthusiasm is aflame, and the tide of events runs high, let the work be finished effectually. Leave no root of bitterness to spring up and work fresh misery to your children. It is a mighty task, indeed, to reorganize the industry not only of four millions of the colored race, but of five millions of whites. Nevertheless, the vast progress you have made in the short space of twenty months fills us with hope that every stain on your freedom will shortly be removed, and that the erasure of that foul blot upon civilization and Christianity—chattel slavery—during your Presidency will cause the name of Abraham Lincoln to be honored and revered by posterity. We are certain that such a glorious consummation will cement Great Britain to the United States in close and enduring regards. Our interests, moreover, are identified with yours. We are truly one people, though locally separate. And if you have any ill-wishers here, be assured they are chiefly those who oppose liberty at home, and that they will be powerless to stir up quarrels between us, from the very day in which your country becomes, undeniably and without exception, the home of the free. Accept our high admiration of your firmness in upholding the proclamation of freedom.

January, 1863.

PRESIDENT LINCOLN'S LETTER
TO THE CITIZENS OF MANCHESTER, ENGLAND.

MANCHESTER, FEBRUARY 10, 1863

The following letter and inclosure were received yesterday by the Mayor of Manchester, Abel Heywood, Esq.:

LEGATION OF THE UNITED STATES,
LONDON, FEBRUARY 9, 1863.

Sir: I have the honor to transmit to you, by the hands of Mr. Moran, the Assistant Secretary of this Legation, a letter of the President of the United States, addressed to you as chairman of the meeting of workingmen, held at Manchester, on the thirty-first of December, and in acknowledgment of the address which I had the pleasure to forward from that meeting.

I am, sir, your obedient servant,

CHARLES FRANCIS ADAMS

Abel Heywood, Esq.
Chairman, etc., Manchester.

Executive Mansion, Washington, January 18, 1863.

To the Workingmen of Manchester:

I have the honor to acknowledge the receipt of the address and resolutions which you sent me on the eve of the new year.

When I came on the fourth of March, 1861, through a free and constitutional election, to preside in the Government of the United States, the country was found at the verge of civil war. Whatever might have been the cause, or whosesoever the fault, one duty, paramount to all others, was before me, namely, to maintain and preserve at once the Constitution and the integrity of the Federal Republic. A conscientious purpose to perform this duty is the key to all the measures of administration which have been, and to all which will hereafter be pursued. Under our frame of government and my official oath, I could not depart from this purpose if I would. It is not always in the power of governments to enlarge or restrict the scope of moral results which follow the policies that they may deem it necessary, for the public safety, from time to time to adopt.

I have understood well that the duty of self-preservation rests solely with the American people. But I have at the same time been aware that favor or disfavor of foreign nations might have a material influence in enlarging and prolonging the struggle with disloyal men in which the country is engaged. A fair examination of history has seemed to authorize a belief that the past action and influences of the United States were generally regarded as having been beneficial toward mankind. I have, therefore, reckoned upon the forbearance of nations. Circumstances—to some of which you kindly allude—induced me especially to expect that, if justice and good faith should be practised by the United States, they would encounter no hostile influence on the part of Great Britain. It is now a pleasant duty to acknowledge the demonstration you have given of your desire that a spirit of peace and amity toward this country may prevail in the councils of your Queen, who is respected and esteemed in your own country only more than she is by the kindred nation which has its home on this side of the Atlantic.

I know, and deeply deplore, the sufferings which the workingmen at Manchester, and in all Europe, are called to endure in this crisis. It has been often and studiously represented that the attempt to overthrow this Government, which was built upon the foundation of human rights, and to substitute for it one which should rest exclusively on the basis of human slavery, was likely to obtain the favor of Europe. Through the action of our disloyal citizens, the workingmen of Europe have been subjected to severe trial, for the purpose of forcing their sanction to that attempt. Under these circumstances I cannot but regard your decisive utterances upon the question as an instance of sublime Christian heroism which has not been surpassed in any age or in any country. It is indeed an energetic and reinspiring assurance of the inherent power of truth, and of the ultimate and universal triumph of justice, humanity, and freedom. I do not doubt that the sentiments you have expressed will be sustained by your great nation; and, on the other hand, I have no hesitation in assuring you that they will excite admiration, esteem, and the most reciprocal feelings of friendship among the American people. I hail this interchange of sentiment, therefore, as an augury that, whatever else may happen, whatever misfortune may befall your country or my own, the peace and friendship which now exist between the two nations will be, as it shall be my desire to make them, perpetual.

ABRAHAM LINCOLN.

15

Abraham Lincoln, The Emancipation Proclamation, January 1, 1863

In spite of conservative protests, Lincoln issued the Emancipation Proclamation on January 1, 1863 (*Alternatives 3, 4, and 9*). Secretary of the Treasury Salmon P. Chase suggested the concluding paragraph.

Document†

The Emancipation Proclamation.

by the President of the United States of America—A Proclamation.

Whereas, on the twenty-second day of September, in the year of our Lord one thousand eight hundred and sixty-two, a proclamation was issued by the President of the United States containing among other things the following, to wit:

"That on the first day of January, in the year of our Lord one thousand eight hundred and sixty-three, all persons held as slaves within any State, or designated part of a State, the people whereof shall then be in rebellion against the United States, shall be then, thenceforth and forever free, and the Executive Government of the United States, including the military and naval authorities thereof, will recognize and maintain the freedom of such persons, and will do no act or acts to repress such persons, or any of them, in any efforts they may make for their actual freedom.

"That the Executive will, on the first day of January aforesaid, by proclamation, designate the States and parts of States, if any, in which the people therein respectively shall then be in rebellion against the United States, and the fact that any State, or the people thereof, shall on that day be in good faith represented in the Congress of the United States by members chosen thereto, at elections wherein a majority of the qualified voters of such States shall have participated, shall, in the absence of strong contervailing testimony, be deemed conclusive evidence that such State and the people thereof are not then in rebellion against the United States."

†From: Frank Moore, ed., *Rebellion Record*, vol. VI, part II, pp. 207-08.

Now, therefore, I, Abraham Lincoln, President of the United States, by virtue of the power in me vested as Commander-in-chief of the Army and Navy of the United States in time of actual armed rebellion against the authority and Government of the United States, and as a fit and necessary war measure for suppressing said rebellion, do, on this first day of January, in the year of our Lord one thousand eight hundred and sixty-three, and in accordance with my purpose so to do, publicly proclaimed for the full period of one hundred days from the day of the first above-mentioned order, and designate, as the States and parts of States wherein the people thereof respectively are this day in rebellion against the United States, the following, to wit: Arkansas, Texas, Louisiana, except the parishes of St. Bernard, Plaquemines, Jefferson, St. John, St. Charles, St. James, Ascension, Assumption, Terre Bonne, Lafourche St. Mary, St. Martin, and Orleans, including the City of New-Orleans. Mississippi, Alabama, Florida, Georgia, South-Carolina, North-Carolina and Virginia, except the forty-eight counties designated as West-Virginia, and also the counties of Berkeley, Accomac, Northampton, Elizabeth City, York, Princess Ann, and Norfolk, including the cities of Norfolk and Portsmouth, and which excepted parts are, for the present, left precisely as if this proclamation were not issued.

And by virtue of the power and for the purpose aforesaid, I do order and declare that all persons held as slaves within said designated States and parts of States are, and henceforward shall be free; and that the Executive Government of the United States, including the Military and Naval authorities thereof, will recognize and maintain the freedom of said persons.

And I hereby enjoin upon the people so declared to be free, to abstain from all violence, unless in necessary self-defence, and I recommend to them, that in all cases, when allowed, they labor faithfully for reasonable wages.

And I further declare and make known that such persons of suitable condition will be received into the armed service of the United States to garrison forts, positions, stations, and other places, and to man vessels of all sorts in said service.

And upon this, sincerely believed to be an act of justice, warranted by the Constitution, upon military necessity, I invoke the considerate judgment of mankind and the gracious favor of Almighty God.

In witness whereof, I have hereunto set my hand and caused the seal of the United States to be affixed.

[L. S.]   Done at the City of Washington, this first day of January, in the year of our Lord one thousand eight hundred and sixty-three, and of the Independence of the United States of America the eighty-seventh.

ABRAHAM LINCOLN.
By the President—William H. Seward,
Secretary of State.

part two

B. Historians' Selections

16

T. Harry Williams, Lincoln and the Radicals

Professor T. Harry Williams of Louisiana State University has written the standard account about Lincoln's relations with the radicals. Emphasizing the differences between the president and the outspokenly antislavery wing of the Republican party, he represents a school of thought which stresses Lincoln's reluctant espousal of emancipation as a result of radical pressure.

Document†

The Jacobins had forced Lincoln to take the general they wanted—a man who would fight and who believed in the radical war aims. Visions of greater victories haunted their minds. They dreamed of filling all the commands with radical officers, and of proclamations of emancipation issuing on every hand. And at the same time they scored another resounding triumph over the administration by pushing through Congress measures directed at the destruction of slavery. Steadily the Jacobin machine was seizing the control of the Republican Party, and Lincoln's hopes of a nonpartisan coalition faded rapidly. The weeks of July were spacious days for radicalism.

An obscure Republican congressman from Maine furnished the Jacobins with a slogan to inscribe on their banner as they drove to conquest. Speaking in the House in February, Frederick A. Pike shouted: "Our duty to-day is to tax and fight. Twin brothers of great power; to them in good time shall be added a third; and whether he shall be of executive parentage, or generated in Congress, or spring, like Minerva, full-grown from the head of our Army, I care not. Come he will, and his name shall be Emancipation. And these three—Tax, Fight, and Emancipate—shall be the Trinity of our salvation. In this sign we shall conquer."

Unfortunately for the radicals, Pike's enunciation of the dogma of the Jacobin faith did not move Lincoln. Not only did he refuse to be converted and repent of his sins, but he stubbornly denied the third part of the Trinity.

†From: T. Harry Williams, *Lincoln and the Radicals* (Madison, Wis.: The University of Wisconsin Press; copyright © 1941 by The Regents of the University of Wisconsin), pp. 156-158, 168-170. Reprinted by permission of the University of Wisconsin Press. Footnotes omitted.

To the disgust of the radicals he still persisted in worshipping a false god—his policy of a conservative coalition party with but one purpose, the restoration of the Union. He did take one step toward the radical altar, but it was a timid one; and the Jacobins, who demanded an enthusiastic convert or none, repulsed him. Lincoln had always been an advocate of gradual, compensated emancipation, to be accomplished by the only method he considered constitutional—through voluntary action by the states in which slavery existed. Now on March 6 he proposed such a scheme to Congress, largely for the purpose of conciliating the rising antislavery spirit which the radicals were whipping up in the country. Stressing that gradual emancipation was "better for all," he recommended that the government cooperate with any state wishing to free its slaves by providing "pecuniary aid"—in other words, compensation.

Congress passed a bill embodying Lincoln's ideas. But the measure failed to achieve any practical results, primarily because the loyal Border States in which Lincoln hoped to start the process were opposed to any federal interference with their domestic institutions. Nor did the president win over the Jacobins; they were bitterly contemptuous of his scheme. Stevens dismissed it as "about the most diluted, milk and water gruel proposition that was ever given to the American nation." John Hickman thought Lincoln was in reality trying to protect slavery and was offering "a compensation to the North for disappointed hopes." The fiery Pennsylvanian denounced Lincoln's plan as "rather a palliative and caution than an open and avowed policy; it is rather an excuse for non-action than an avowed determination to act. . . . Neither the message nor the resolution is manly and open. They are both covert and insidious. . . ."

Abraham Lincoln caught the significance of events in those hot July days when the spirit of radicalism burgeoned in the nation and the Jacobins in Congress wrenched from him the control of the Republican Party. He knew at last that the radicals represented an implacable force which he could not ignore and to which perhaps he must yield. On July 10, while driving to the funeral of Stanton's infant son, he confided to Seward and Welles, who were in the carriage with him, that he had decided to issue a proclamation of freedom. And on the twenty-second he startled the other members of the Cabinet by reading to them the draft of an edict freeing the slaves in the rebellious states. He would have given it to the country immediately, had not Seward argued that the moment was not propitious. Wait for a military victory, he urged, otherwise the proclamation would impress the world as a shriek of despair from an expiring government. Lincoln saw the wisdom of this advice. He put the document aside and looked about for a general who could win him a triumph. At this moment John Pope was shouting that if he had the Army of the Potomac he would march into Richmond.

Other reasons than fear of the Jacobins helped mold Lincoln's decision to free the slaves by executive action. Undoubtedly he had in mind the critical foreign situation: certain European countries were on the verge of extending diplomatic recognition to the Confederacy. In England and France the liberal parties favored the Union cause; they believed the North was fighting the battle of democracy against aristocracy. But they found it difficult to justify their position when the government of the United States proclaimed again and again that its only purpose in waging war was to restore the Union. Lincoln knew that a bold declaration of an antislavery policy would rally the European liberals and inspire them to oppose any friendly gestures by their governments toward the Confederacy. But bulking larger in Lincoln's thoughts than the uncertainties of diplomatic developments were the grave issues of domestic politics. The strongest cornerstone of his program had been the all-parties coalition of Republicans, Democrats, and loyal slaveholders, to fight the war to a conclusion. To hold this discordant conglomeration together it was imperative that he be able to repress the abolitionist instincts of his own party. This Lincoln could not do. Every time the Republicans, the dominant and most numerous element in the combination, moved toward radicalism, the other factions took fright and drew away. And in the summer of 1862 the Republican Party was rapidly going radical. The Confiscation Act, repudiating the purposes of the war as defined in the Crittenden Resolution, smashed Lincoln's plan beyond repair. He had lost the Border States and many of the conservatives. There remained only the Republicans. And while he had hoped to build an inclusive political alliance to sustain his efforts to restore the Union, it was important above all else that he have the support of his own ardent followers. Without their aid he could not preserve the American experiment in government. Nor was he blind to the mounting Jacobinism among the people whose tribune he always considered himself to be. If they demanded that the Union be saved through emancipation, Abraham Lincoln would save it that way.

17

Hans L. Trefousse, The Radical Republicans

T. Harry Williams' interpretation has been modified by David Donald, whose views influenced a later school of historians. Arguing that Lincoln and the radicals often cooperated, Hans L. Trefousse has emphasized the essential points of agreement in long term aims between the president and his critics. According to this interpretation, Lincoln utilized existing radical pressure to carry out emancipation policies which he himself was not unwilling to undertake.

Document†

Just as Lincoln worked with the radicals in first spurring on and then removing McClellan, so he also cooperated with them in the most controversial issue of the time: the problem of emancipation. Cognizant of the unpopularity of abolitionism and its varieties in the North and determined to retain the loyalty of the border states, at first he sought to exclude it from consideration. But if there was one tenet upon which all radicals agreed it was their demand for an unrelenting war upon slavery. They even maintained that it was impossible to win without it. How Lincoln eventually adopted their point of view without at the same time completely alienating conservatives in the North and the border states was a good illustration of the relationship between the President and the ultras. . . .

The President's own position on slavery was in fact not as different from the radicals' as has sometimes been assumed. The man who, as early as 1858, had said, "I have always hated slavery, I think as much as any abolitionist," and who, fourteen years after the event, vividly remembered the torment the sight of shackled Negroes on a steamship had caused him as a young man, was no archconservative. He had often expressed his detestation of the institution and his hopes that it would soon disappear. But he knew that it was essential to maintain the nation's unity; the unpopularity of abolition in the North had not abated; nor were the border states entirely secure. In the initiation of antislavery measures, he would have to move with care, relying on his own sense of timing rather than on the impetuous demands of his extremist

†From: *The Radical Republicans: Lincoln's Vanguard for Racial Justice*, by Hans L. Trefousse. Copyright © 1968 by Hans L. Trefousse. (New York: Alfred A. Knopf, 1969), pp. 203, 208-09, 229. Footnotes omitted. Reprinted by permission of Alfred A. Knopf, Inc.

advisers. Nevertheless, their pressure was useful; nobody knew better than he how to harness it for the purposes of human progress to which he himself was committed. . . .

Whether Lincoln would have been willing or able to issue the proclamation without radical prodding, however, is questionable. Confronted with difficulties, dubious about his own constitutional powers, and anxious to avoid offense to the border states, the President needed the ultras' help in order to commit himself. "In Lincoln's desk the Emancipation Proclamation would probably have remained had it not been for the increased activities of the radicals. . . ," William Best Hesseltine, a historian by no means sympathetic to the ultras, has written, and his conclusion is supported by the evidence. As Julian, a contemporary observer, reminisced afterwards, "It was in yielding to this [radical] pressure that he finally became the liberator of the slaves through the triumph of our arms which ensued." And considering the relationship between Lincoln and Thaddeus Stevens, perhaps one of the most representative radicals in the House, Alexander K. McClure, the Pennsylvania newspapermen, stated: "Had Stevens not declared for the abolition of slavery as soon as the war began, and pressed it in and out of season, Lincoln would not have issued his Emancipation Proclamation as early as September, 1862." Carl Schurz, also remembering Lincoln's dependence on the radicals, was particularly impressed with Sumner's influence. He wrote:

> Lincoln regarded and esteemed Sumner as the outspoken conscience of the advanced anti-slavery sentiment, the confidence and hearty cooperation of which was to him of the highest moment in the common struggle. While it required all his fortitude to bear Sumner's intractable insistence, Lincoln did not at all deprecate Sumner's agitation for an immediate emancipation policy, even though it did reflect upon the course of the administration. On the contrary, he rather welcomed everything that would prepare the public mind for the approaching development.

18

Benjamin Quarles, Lincoln and the Negro

Benjamin Quarles's book on Lincoln and the Negro is the definitive work on the subject. Carefully tracing the president's developing thought on race relations, Professor Quarles demonstrates Lincoln's capacity to grow. The following excerpts contain the author's analysis of the factors that led the president to issue the Emancipation Proclamation.

Document†

Entering into Lincoln's deliberation and fixing his determination about issuing an emancipation proclamation were considerations of a varied nature—military, political, and diplomatic. To Lincoln the first of these was pre-eminent: military necessity required that the enemy be deprived of his slaves. Lincoln knew that the black population of the South was one of its greatest assets. The Confederacy had not actually put a gun in the hands of the colored man, but tens of thousands of its slaves saw front-line service, being employed as orderlies, teamsters, and military laborers. Slaves who remained on the home front supplied the skills for the factories and the brawn for working the mines. And it was the labor of the plantation slave that produced the cotton the South hoped to sell in England. To weaken this black arm of the Confederacy had become the first order of military business, a blunt fact from which Lincoln could not flinch.

In the late summer of 1863 (on September 2), Lincoln told Secretary Chase that the Emancipation Proclamation had been issued solely as a military necessity and not because it was politically expedient or morally right. Nonetheless, political considerations had influenced the issuing of the edict. Himself a Republican, Lincoln was obliged to make concessions to the point of view of his party, including its Radical wing. As the war went on with no end in sight, these Radicals became more insistent than ever that the abolition of slavery become an officially avowed goal of the war. The support

†From: *Lincoln and the Negro*, by Benjamin Quarles (New York: Oxford University Press, 1962), pp. 134-39. Copyright © 1962 by Oxford University Press, Inc. Reprinted by permission.

of these Radicals was important to the Lincoln administration, and this support could be jeopardized without an edict of emancipation.

By the late summer of 1862 there were signs, as the politically astute Lincoln could see, that the Radical point of view on slavery was gaining strength. John W. Forney's *Philadelphia Press* carried a pointed editorial in its issue of July 30, 1862:

> A million able-bodied men await but our word to ally themselves with us bodily, as they are with us in heart. A magnificent black blister as a counter irritant! A guerrilla power such as the world has never seen.

Such a point of view Lincoln might take in stride if uttered by an abolitionist or even by a Republican congressman. But the *Philadelphia Press* was such a defender of the Lincoln administration as to be considered an organ of the White House. When influential Lincoln men like Forney joined the emancipation chorus, no soothsayer of political behavior need be summoned to tell of tomorrow.

The extent to which political considerations shaped the issuing of the emancipation edict becomes evident in Lincoln's dealings with the Altoona Conference governors. Andrew G. Curtin of Pennsylvania and John A. Andrew of Massachusetts had called a meeting of loyal governors to be held at Altoona, Pennsylvania, during the last week of September 1862. As announced in the call, the chief aim of the conference was to press for action against slavery. Lincoln was not asleep. By a shrewd stroke he proceeded to undercut the scheduled conference. He summoned governors Curtin and Andrew to the White House and told them of the emancipation proclamation lying in his desk awaiting a battlefield victory. Curtin and Andrew realized that they had been outflanked; they had also been won over.

Fortunately for Lincoln, the victory at Antietam enabled him to issue his proclamation before the Altoona meeting. After their conference the governors came to Washington in a group and called at the White House on September 26. They congratulated Lincoln on the issuing of the proclamation, and Lincoln, with a straightfaced solemnity matching theirs, told them that their approval of the measure assured him, more than anything else, that he had done the right thing.

A third important factor in bringing about and supporting the proclamation was European, particularly English, opinion. In England the governing and aristocratic classes were anti-North and would have been glad to extend diplomatic recognition to the Confederacy. But the masses and the middle class in the British Isles were Union sympathizers and disliked the South as slavery's strongest bastion in the Western world.

In large measure the groundwork for this British antislavery sentiment had been laid by American Negroes who for a quarter of a century had been touring England, Ireland, and Scotland. Many of these Negroes were escaped slaves, like William Wells Brown, who in five years abroad made over a thousand addresses. William and Ellen Craft moved British audiences to tears with the story of their dramatic escape from Macon, Georgia, with Ellen disguised as a young slavemaster.

The procession of Negroes did not abate with the war. American Negroes like J. Sella Martin acted almost as if they were ministers without portfolio in furthering the Union cause. Far from her Salem, Massachusetts, home, the young, eloquent, and earnest Sarah P. Remond, always effective on the platform, exhorted her listeners to stand firm:

> Let no diplomacy of statesmen, no intimidation of slaveholders, no scarcity of cotton, no fear of slave insurrections, prevent the people of Great Britain from maintaining their position as the friend of the oppressed Negro.

The greatest drawing card among the American Negroes during the autumn of 1862 was William Andrew Davis, the escaped ex-coachman of Confederate President Jefferson Davis. These Negroes, like their counterparts before the war, did much to intensify the antislavery sentiment of the British masses.

Lincoln knew that reformist groups and workingmen's associations in England would hail an edict of emancipation. He was aware, too, that such a proclamation would be a heavy blow to the foreign policy of the Confederacy, striking "King Cotton diplomacy" in a most vulnerable spot. After the Emancipation Proclamation was issued, the Confederate agents stationed in European capitals were no longer able to play down the slavery issue by asserting that the North had no intention of changing the status of the black man.

"I did not know," wrote Lincoln's friend, Pennsylvania politician Alexander K. McClure, "and few were permitted to know, the importance of an Emancipation policy in restraining the recognition of the Confederacy by France and England." Equally emphatic on this point was one who did happen to be in the know—the Secretary of State. It was not alone the clamor at home, said Seward on January 22, 1863, that induced Lincoln to issue the proclamation. He had been influenced also "by the wishes of foreign Nations," who "were urging that the slaves should be declared free."

Lincoln did not underestimate the role the proclamation would play across the Atlantic. It enabled abolitionist groups like the London Emancipation Society to cry out that "the South is fighting for slavery, whilst the North is fully committed to the destruction of slavery." Like other antislavery organizations abroad, the London group was given a fresh impetus by Lincoln's edict, enlarging its program and personnel. Beginning in December 1862 and running through the following March, more than fifty well-attended public meetings in support of Lincoln's proclamation were held in the major cities of Great Britain and Ireland.

At each of these gatherings the chief order of business was the drafting of a resolution or an address to Lincoln, to be sent to him through the offices of the American ambassador to the Court of St. James. During the first weeks of 1863 Charles Francis Adams was kept busy receiving these resolutions, arranging them in batches, and forwarding them to Seward. Diplomatic pouches containing such resolutions of approval were mailed by Adams on January 22, February 5, February 12, and February 19. In the letter accompanying the February 19 mailing, Adams informed Seward that "the current of popular sentiment flows with little abatement of strength." The ambassador made bold to add that he was sure that Lincoln was unprepared "for the multiplication of addresses, from various quarters, which has ensued."

Seward asked Adams, in a letter of February 25, to find some way "of communicating the President's grateful responses" to those who had "generously addressed him concerning our affairs." Seward knew that Lincoln could never personally answer more than a handful of these impressive sets of resolutions, which sometimes bore hundreds of signatures, but he also knew that Lincoln did not wish to have his British supporters go unthanked.

Member of Parliament and reformer Richard Cobden, who was interested in free men as well as free trade, was sure that Lincoln's edict turned the tide of public opinion in the British Isles. "You know," he wrote to Charles Sumner from London's Athenaeum Club on February 13, 1863, "how much alarmed I was from the first lest our government should interpose in your affairs ... This state of feeling existed up to the announcement of the President's emancipation Policy. From that moment our old antislavery feeling began to arouse itself, and it has been gathering strength ever since."

Having previously weighed the major factors for issuing the preliminary proclamation, Lincoln was not likely to withhold the final edict. In setting the date for January 1, 1863, he had shown a good sense of the propitious moment. From the beginning he had been his own preacher, knowing that there was a time to wait, a time to warn, and a time to consummate. And now with the war about to enter its third calendar year, the North was ready to accept the Lincoln point of view that it was necessary to declare the rebel slaves free if the Union was to be saved. "In reference to the Proclamation of Old Abe's," wrote Illinois infantryman Michael Gapen to his sister from his campsite on Yacona Creek, Mississippi, on December 17, 1862, "I did not like it at first myself, but I have now come to the conclusion that it is the best thing that can possibly be done." Two days earlier the House of Representatives, reflecting grassroots sentiment, voted 78 to 52 in favor of a resolution supporting the Lincoln proclamation as a measure warranted to hasten the restoration of peace.

Lincoln never had any intention of withholding the final proclamation. True, the policy of emancipation may have originally been thrust upon him; but by the time he announced it to the world, it had become an integral part of his own thinking. Spiritualists might claim that Lincoln issued the edict upon the advice of mediums, and reformist and political groups might lay claim to having stiffened his backbone. Lincoln would not have bothered to dispute these claims, for he was secure in the knowledge that the decision had become his own.

19

John Hope Franklin, The Emancipation Proclamation

The standard work on the Emancipation Proclamation is the book by Professor John Hope Franklin of the University of Chicago. Analyzing the factors which contributed to the president's decision and its results, the author, substantially agreeing with Quarles, brings out the mixed motives that led Lincoln to chose the option he did.

Document†

The character of the Civil War could not possibly have been the same after the President issued the Emancipation Proclamation as it had been before January 1, 1863. During the first twenty months of the war, no one had been more careful than Lincoln himself to define the war merely as one to save the Union. He did this not only because such a definition greatly simplified the struggle and kept the border states fairly loyal, but also because he deeply felt that this was the only legitimate basis for prosecuting the war. When, therefore, he told Horace Greeley that if he could save the Union without freeing a single slave he made the clearest possible statement of his fundamental position. And he was holding to this position despite the fact that he had written the first draft of the Emancipation Proclamation at least six weeks before he wrote his reply to Greeley's famous "Prayer of Twenty Millions."

Lincoln saw no contradiction between the contents of his reply to Greeley and the contents of the Emancipation Proclamation. For he had come to the conclusion that in order to save the Union he must emancipate *some* of the slaves. His critics were correct in suggesting that the Proclamation was a rather frantic measure, an act of last resort. By Lincoln's own admission it was, indeed, a desperate act; for the prospects of Union success were not bright. He grabbed at the straw of a questionable victory at Antietam as the occasion for issuing the Preliminary Proclamation. If anything convinced him in late December that he should go through with issuing the final Proclamation, it was the ignominious defeat of the Union forces at Fredericksburg. *Something* needed to be done. Perhaps the Emancipation Proclamation would turn the trick!

†From: *The Emancipation Proclamation*, by John Hope Franklin (Garden City, N.Y.: Doubleday and Co., Inc., 1963), pp. 136-43. Footnotes omitted. Copyright © 1963 by John Hope Franklin. Reprinted by permission of Doubleday & Co., Inc.

The language of the Proclamation revealed no significant modification of the aims of the war. Nothing was clearer than the fact that Lincoln was taking the action under his authority "as Commander-in-Chief of the Army and Navy." The situation that caused him to take the action was that there was an "actual armed rebellion against the authority and government of the United States." He regarded the Emancipation Proclamation, therefore, as "a fit and necessary war measure for suppressing said rebellion." In another place in the Proclamation he called on the military and naval authorities to recognize and maintain the freedom of the slaves. Finally the President declared, in the final paragraph of the Proclamation, that the measure was "warranted by the Constitution upon military necessity." This was, indeed, a war measure, conceived and promulgated to put down the rebellion and save the Union.

Nevertheless, both by what it said and what it did not say, the Proclamation greatly contributed to the significant shift in 1863 in the way the war was regarded. It recognized the right of emancipated slaves to defend their freedom. The precise language was that they should "abstain from all violence, unless in necessary self-defence." It also provided that former slaves could now be received into the armed services. While it was clear that they were to fight to save the Union, the fact remained that since their own fate was tied to that of the Union, they would also be fighting for their own freedom. The Negro who, in December 1862, could salute his own colonel instead of blacking the boots of a Confederate colonel, as he had been doing a year earlier, had a stake in the war that was not difficult to define. However loyal to the Union the Negro troops were—and they numbered some 190,000 by April 1865—one is inclined to believe that they were fighting primarily for freedom for themselves and their brothers in the months that followed the issuance of the Emancipation Proclamation.

Despite the fact that the President laid great stress on the issuance of the Proclamation as a military necessity, he did not entirely overlook the moral and humanitarian significance of the measure. And even in the document itself he gave some indication of his appreciation of this particular dimension that was, in time, to eclipse many other considerations. He said that the emancipation of the slaves was "sincerely believed to be an act of justice." This conception of emancipation could hardly be confined to the slaves in states or parts of states that were in rebellion against the United States on January 1, 1863. It must be recalled, moreover, that in the same sentence that he referred to emancipation as an "act of justice" he invoked "the considerate judgment of mankind and the gracious favor of Almighty God." This raised the Proclamation above the level of just another measure for the effective prosecution of the war. And, in turn, the war became more than a war to save the integrity and independence of the Union. It became also a war to promote the freedom of mankind.

Throughout the previous year the President had held to the view that Negroes should be colonized in some other part of the world. And he advanced this view with great vigor wherever and whenever possible. He pressed the Cabinet and Congress to accept and implement his colonization views, and he urged Negroes to realize that it was best for all concerned that they should leave the United States. It is not without significance that Lincoln omitted from the Emancipation Proclamation any reference to colonization. It seems clear that the President had abandoned hope of gaining support for his scheme or of persuading Negroes to leave the only home they knew. Surely, moreover, it would have been a most incongruous policy as well as an ungracious act to have asked Negroes to perform one of the highest acts of citizenship—fighting for their country—and then invite them to leave. Thus, by inviting Negroes into the armed services and omitting all mention of colonization, the President indicated in the Proclamation that Negroes would enjoy a status that went beyond mere freedom. They were to be free persons, fighting for their *own* country, a country in which they were to be permitted to remain.

The impact of the Proclamation on slavery and Negroes was profound. Negroes looked upon it as a document of freedom, and they made no clear distinction between the areas affected by the Proclamation and those not affected by it. One has the feeling that the interest of the contrabands in Washington in seeing whether their home counties were excepted or included in the Proclamation was an academic interest so far as their own freedom was concerned. After all, they had proclaimed their own freedom and had put themselves beyond the force of the slave law or their masters. The celebration of the issuance of the Proclamation by thousands of Negroes in Norfolk illustrates the pervasive influence of the document. President Lincoln had said that Norfolk slaves were not emancipated by his Proclamation. Norfolk Negroes, however, ignored the exception and welcomed the Proclamation as the instrument of their own deliverance.

Slavery, in or out of the Confederacy, could not possibly have survived the Emancipation Proclamation. Slaves themselves, already restive under their yoke and walking off the plantation in many places, were greatly encouraged upon learning that Lincoln wanted them to be free. They proceeded to oblige him. There followed what one authority has called a general strike and another has described as widespread slave disloyalty throughout the Confederacy. Lincoln understood the full implications of the Proclamation. That is one of the reasons why he delayed issuing it as long as he did. Once the power of the government was enlisted on the side of freedom in one place, it could not successfully be restrained from supporting freedom in some other place. It was too fine a distinction to make. Not even the slaveholders in the excepted areas could make it. They knew, therefore, that the Emancipation Proclamation was the beginning of the end of slavery for them. Many of them did not like it, but the realities of the situation clearly indicated what the future had in store for them.

The critics of the Lincoln Administration stepped up their attack after January 1, 1863, because they fully appreciated the fact that the Proclamation changed the character of the war. Orestes A. Brownson, Clement L. Vallandigham, William C. Fowler, Samuel S. Cox, and others insisted that the Proclamation represented a new policy that made impossible any hasty conclusion of the struggle based on a compromise. The President had become the captive of the abolitionists who had persuaded him to change the war aims from preservation of the Union to abolition of slavery. Some of them, such as Vallandigham, were proslavery and openly defended the "peculiar institution" against what they called unconstitutional interference. Others, such as Fowler, felt that the question of slavery was extraneous and the introduction of emancipation into the picture was an act so loathesome as to be virtually criminal. All agreed that the Proclamation transformed the war into something to which they were even more bitterly opposed than they had been to the war to save the Union.

If the abolitionists had gained ascendancy in the councils of the President, they were not altogether satisfied with the results of their influence. For months on end, they had been imploring the President to abolish slavery. "Stevens, Sumner, and Wilson simply haunt me with their importunities for a Proclamation of Emancipation," Lincoln complained to a friend in 1862. Outright emancipation of all the slaves, without compensation or colonization and without apologies for it as a military necessity, was what the abolitionists wanted. "Patch up a compromise now," warned Thaddeus Stevens, "leaving this germ of evil and it will soon again overrun the whole South, even if you free three fourths of the slaves. Your peace would be a curse. You would have expended countless treasures and untold lives in vain." Many abolitionists agreed with Stevens, when he said, in early September 1862, that no one in the government seemed to have the moral courage to take the necessary steps to abolish slavery.

In the light of the demands they had been making, the language of the Emancipation Proclamation could hardly have been the source of unrestrained joy on the part of the abolitionists. The Proclamation did not represent the spirit of "no compromise" that had characterized their stand for a generation. There was no emancipation in the border states, with which the abolitionists had so little patience. Parts of states that were under Union control were excepted, much to the dismay of the abolitionists, whose view was ably set forth by Chase. Obviously, the President was not completely under their sway, despite the claims of numerous critics of the Administration. For the most part, the Proclamation represented Lincoln's views. It was in no sense the result of abolitionist dictation.

And yet, when the Proclamation finally came, the abolitionists displayed a remarkable capacity for accommodating themselves to what was, from their point of view, an obvious compromise. Some of them took credit for the begrudging concessions that the compromise represented. They were wrung, Wendell Phillips told a Boston audience, "from reluctant leaders by the determined heart of the masses." A few weeks later he said to a group of New Yorkers, "Possess your souls in patience, not as having already attained, not as if we were already perfect, but because the whole nation, as one man, has for more than a year set its face Zionward. Ever since September 22nd of last year, the nation has turned its face Zionward, and ever since Burnside drew his sword in Virginia, we have moved toward that point.... We have found at last the method, and we are in earnest."

Other abolitionists had even fewer reservations. Thaddeus Stevens praised Lincoln's Proclamation. It contained "precisely the principles which I had advocated," he told his Pennsylvania constituents. For thirty years William Lloyd Garrison had never been known to make concessions as far as slavery was concerned. Yet, he declared the Emancipation Proclamation to be a measure that should take its place along with the Declaration of Independence as one of the nation's truly important historic documents. Frederick Douglass, the leading Negro abolitionist, said that the Proclamation changed everything. "It gave a new direction to the councils of the Cabinet, and to the conduct of the national arms." Douglass realized that the Proclamation did not extend liberty throughout the land, as the abolitionists hoped, but he took it "for a little more than it purported, and saw in its spirit a life and power far beyond its letter. Its meaning to me was the entire abolition of slavery," he concluded, "and I saw that its moral power would extend much further."

20

Ralph Korngold, Thaddeus Stevens

The point of view that Lincoln delayed rather than furthered emancipation is well represented by Ralph Korngold in his biography of Thaddeus Stevens. Agreeing with T. Harry Williams in judging Lincoln to have been essentially conservative, the author differs from his predecessor in sympathizing not with the president but with Thaddeus Stevens of Pennsylvania, the radical leader of the House of Representatives.

Document†

Lincoln merits the title of Great Emancipator posterity has conferred upon him. He merits it for his unshakable determination to preserve the Union when Garrison, Phillips, Greeley, and other antislavery leaders were in favor of not opposing secession. He merits it for his decision not to evacuate Fort Sumter against the advice of so confirmed an antislavery advocate as Secretary Chase. All this, however, does not alter the fact that reliable evidence shows him to have issued the proclamation not because he considered it desirable from the military or social viewpoint, but from fear of what an exasperated Congress might do when it reassembled in December, 1862. Nor does it alter the fact that although he himself had serious doubts concerning the postwar validity of the proclamation, he continued to exert every possible effort to get the border states to adopt gradual emancipation. Yet he must have known that had his advice been followed, ratification of a constitutional amendment abolishing slavery throughout the republic would have been impossible and the freedom of the slaves would have been dependent upon a court decision. Only when he finally realized that his efforts could not succeed did he declare himself in favor of the amendment.

2

Was it mere coincidence that the President should have made a proposal to Congress for compensated gradual emancipation with federal aid on March 6, 1862—four days before the Article of War forbidding the military to return fugitive slaves was adopted by that body? It will be recalled that Senator

†From: Ralph Korngold, *Thaddeus Stevens, A Being Darkly Wise and Truly Great* (New York: Harcourt, Brace and Co., 1955), pp. 179-85. Footnotes omitted. Reprinted by special permission of Mrs. Ralph Korngold.

Pearce of Maryland had said of that measure: "It is not an act of emancipation in its terms; but so far as it can operate, and does operate, it leads directly to that result." It does not, therefore, appear unreasonable to believe that the President made the proposal in order to arrest, if possible, the congressional drive toward general emancipation the measure portended, and which was to gain momentum during the succeeding months. He proposed the passage of a joint resolution to the effect that the United States would give pecuniary aid to any state that adopted gradual emancipation, "to compensate it for inconvenience, public or private." "In my judgment," he wrote, "gradual and not sudden emancipation is better for all."

Stevens was impatient with Lincoln's proposal. "I have read it over," he said, "and confess I have not been able to see what makes one side so anxious to pass it, or the other so anxious to defeat it. I think it is about the most diluted milk-and-water-gruel proposition that was ever given to the American nation."

He considered general emancipation indispensable and believed the President's proposal only served to delay a measure that would shorten the conflict and save thousands of human lives. Most of all he objected to the following paragraph in the President's message: "Such a proposition on the part of the General Government sets up no claim of a right by the Federal authority to interfere with slavery within State limits—referring as it does the absolute control of the subject, in each case, to the State and the people immediately interested. It is proposed as a matter of perfectly free choice to them."

What was this but a reaffirmation, after a year of insurrection and war, of the President's pronouncement at his inaugural that the federal authority had no legal right to interfere with slavery in the slave states? Stevens repudiated that doctrine, as John Quincy Adams had repudiated it, and as Lincoln himself was to finish by doing. If there never was a time when the federal authority could interfere with slavery in the slave states, then the cause of the rebellion, and of possible future rebellions, could never be eradicated except with the consent of the rebels! What would hinder them from accepting the President's proposal as a matter of expediency and later restoring slavery? That Lincoln himself did not exclude that possibility is evident from the bill he offered to Congress on July 12, 1862, and from the elaboration of his compensated emancipation plan he presented to Congress in December of that year. Both contained a clause dealing with that contingency. The clause in the December document read:

Any State having received bonds as aforesaid, and afterwards reintroducing or tolerating slavery therein, shall refund to the United States the bonds so received, or the value thereof, and all interest paid thereon.

Since in the existing situation emancipation by the slave states themselves could not by the furthest stretch of the imagination have been called "a matter of perfectly free choice," any supposedly voluntary agreement made with them on the matter must necessarily have been of doubtful value.

Stevens did not think such a policy solved anything. He felt that now that the slaveholders had plunged the country into war, the struggle must not cease until its cause had been completely eradicated. "The reunion of the

States must be perfected, and so effected as to remove all causes of disturbance in the future; and to attain this end, it is necessary that the original cause should, if possible, be rooted out." These are Lincoln's words, spoken to a crowd gathered in front of the White House on January 31, 1865. It was the doctrine Stevens preached from the beginning of the war.

The President's proposal was, however, adopted by large majorities in both houses of Congress and approved by him on April 10, 1862. Not wishing to be counted on the side of the proslavery representatives, Stevens abstained from voting.

During the succeeding two months Stevens and the two senators from Massachusetts, Sumner and Wilson, importuned the President to issue an Emancipation Proclamation, but to no avail. Lincoln complained to Senator John B. Henderson of Missouri: "Stevens, Sumner and Wilson haunt me with their importunities for a Proclamation of Emancipation. Where I go and whatever way I turn, they are on my trail, and still in my heart, I have a deep conviction that the hour has not yet come."

On July 12, 1862, the report of the conference committee concerning the second Confiscation Act was accepted by the Senate and the bill was now ready for the President's signature. What must have been the surprise of senators and representatives when on that very day Congress received from the President the draft of a bill, passage of which he recommended, embodying the compensated emancipation proposal, by action of the slave states themselves, he had made four months earlier. The bill specified that pecuniary aid would be given to any state that emancipated its slaves either gradually or immediately, that the aid was to be in the form of interest-bearing bonds, and that the bonds and all interest paid thereon were to be returned if a state "at any time afterwards by law reintroduce or tolerate slavery within its limits."

That the President should have presented the bill to Congress at this juncture is explicable by the fact that it was then his intention to veto the second Confiscation Act. It was therefore in the nature of a counterproposal. The chances that Stevens and his followers would lay aside the act for a renewal of the offer that had proved futile four months earlier were so slim that the President's move must be regarded as a well-nigh desperate attempt to halt the congressional drive toward general emancipation. The bill was referred to committee and never taken up. When one compares this with the vote of 89 to 31 the President's proposal had received in April of that year, one realizes the extent to which Stevens had succeeded in winning over his colleagues. It was no idle boast on his part when he told his constituents at a public meeting at Lancaster in the fall of that year: "In the last week [of the session], after a few remarks of mine, the vote was 84 to 42—84 agreeing with me, when a year ago not fifty could have been found."

The bill was not the President's only attempt to take the rudder from the hands of Stevens and his followers and steer emancipation into what he considered a safer channel. That same day he sought and obtained an interview with the congressional representatives of the border states and addressed them in moving language, imploring them to use every effort so their states would adopt compensated gradual emancipation with federal aid. "I do not speak of emancipation at once," he told them, "but of a decision at once to emancipate gradually. Room in South America for colonization can be obtained cheaply, and in abundance, and when numbers shall be large enough to be company and encouragement for one another, the freed people will not be so reluctant to go."

In his first message to Congress concerning the matter, the President had expressed the opinion that if the border states accepted his proposal, it would deprive the rebel states of the hope that they would ever join them. "This," he had said, "substantially ends the Rebellion." He now repeated: "In my opinion, if you had voted for the resolution in the gradual emancipation Message of last March, the war would now be substantially ended."

No one can read Lincoln's address to the representatives of the border states without profound sympathy for the speaker and an equally profound conviction of the benevolence of his intentions. He believed it to be a task imposed upon him by Providence to restore the Union, but experienced agony of soul at the thought that restoration might prove a curse to the South and to the Negro if general emancipation without colonization was its concomitant.

4

Lincoln had by no means abandoned the hope that the border states might yet adopt compensated gradual emancipation with federal aid, nor the hope that the rebel states might then fall into line and offer to make peace on that basis. He was, therefore, opposed to the second Confiscation Act not only for the reasons he had mentioned in his veto message and to which Congress had given satisfaction in the explanatory joint resolution, but also and especially for a reason he had preferred not to mention: that the act interfered with a solution of the problem he considered far more desirable. He has sometimes been accused of being vacillating. The fact is, however, that when he believed he was right he would stick to his purpose with amazing persistency. His was not the clumsy unyielding stubbornness of his successor Johnson. He would yield, but in such a manner that the advantage usually remained with him.

He had made two attempts to sidetrack the second Confiscation Act—by sending a bill to Congress embodying his compensated gradual emancipation proposal and recommending its adoption, and by making a moving appeal to the representatives of the border states. He must have felt none too sanguine about the success of either of these moves, for since the first of July he had been preparing a third move he meant to make if the two others failed. It was nothing less than a preliminary Emancipation Proclamation serving notice on the rebel states that if they did not lay down their arms by January 1, 1863, he would issue a final proclamation declaring their slaves free. What did this mean? Had Stevens triumphed? Had Lincoln decided to yield? Only apparently so. *The move was obviously intended for the purpose of rendering the second Confiscation Act inoperative for the remainder of that year, since*

the issuing of the preliminary proclamation would fully justify nonenforce-
ment of the act until January, 1863. Thus the *status quo* on slavery would be
maintained for over five months, during which time, the President hoped,
first the border states and then the rebel states might realize the wisdom of
accepting his gradual emancipation proposal. It was a shrewd move that gave
some promise of success. With two such swords of Damocles hanging over
them as enforcement of the second Confiscation Act and a final
Emancipation Proclamation there was reason to believe that the slave states
might weaken, although it is hardly likely that, had they done so, they would
have regarded it as "a matter of perfectly free choice."

21 ═══════════

═══════════ Benjamin P.
Thomas and
Harold M.
Hyman,
Stanton

Benjamin P. Thomas and Harold M. Hyman, in their biography of Edwin M. Stanton, Lincoln's secretary of war, have presented a new view of the reasons for Lincoln's hesitation to publish the Emancipation Proclamation in the summer of 1862. Focusing attention on Chase's actions rather than Seward's, they differ with other authorities and cast some doubt on the accuracy of Carpenter's account (Document 10, above).

Document†
Actually, the President was contemplating a general emancipation as well as the mere employment of a limited number of blacks as soldiers, as he privately advised Stanton. On May 28, Stanton predicted to Sumner that a decree of emancipation would be issued within two months. While driving to the funeral of Stanton's baby with Welles and Seward on July 13, Lincoln brought the emancipation possibility up to them. Welles later remembered Lincoln's saying that this was "the first occasion when he had mentioned the subject to any one." But either Welles's memory played him false or else Lincoln, to prevent jealousy, did not want them to know that Stanton had been his earlier confidant on this subject.

On July 22, the day after Lincoln declined to approve Hunter's request to enlist Negroes, Francis Brockholst Cutting, a New York lawyer who had been a rabid proslavery Democrat, called on Stanton. The Secretary told him that slavery, the cause of sectional troubles, must be wiped out in order to weaken the enemy and to rally the ever increasing number of antislavery people in the North to a more vigorous support of the war effort.

Somewhat to Stanton's surprise, Cutting agreed with him. Stanton asked him if he would be willing to talk to Lincoln—a free expression of opinion from a onetime proslavery Democrat such as Cutting might go far toward convincing the President that loyal Northern Democrats were now more

†From: *Stanton: The Life and Times of Lincoln's Secretary of War,* by Benjamin P. Thomas and Harold M. Hyman (New York: Alfred A. Knopf, Inc., 1962), pp. 238-40. Footnotes omitted. Copyright © 1962 by Alfred A. Knopf, Inc. Reprinted by permission of the publisher.

willing to support an antislavery program than was generally suspected. Cutting readily assented, and Stanton took him to Lincoln's office, where he left the two men alone.

Cutting talked with Lincoln for two hours. He pointed out the desirability of emancipation as a deterrent to recognition of the Confederacy by foreign governments, and the growing impatience of people of antislavery convictions, the group on which Lincoln must chiefly rely for support in winning the war. Lincoln urged the necessity of holding the border states in line. Cutting responded that they could never be relied on and were disloyal at heart; their congressmen would not even accept the offer of compensated emancipation that Lincoln had been urging upon them almost from the beginning of the war. Apparently this meeting which Stanton arranged helped Lincoln reach a fateful decision.

The regular cabinet meeting took place later that day, and the question of arming Negroes was again brought up. "The impression left upon my mind by the whole discussion was," Chase wrote, "that while the President thought that the organization, equipment, and arming of negroes would be productive of more evil than good, he was not unwilling that commanders should, at their discretion, arm for purely defensive purposes, slaves coming within their lines." But on the matter of emancipation Lincoln was now ready to go further than most members of his cabinet had suspected. Taking a sheet of paper from his pocket, he read a proclamation that on January 1, 1863, all slaves in states still in rebellion were to be forever free.

Stanton favored Lincoln's issuing the proclamation at once. Chase, more surprised than anyone, said the measure went beyond anything he had contemplated. He thought it would be better to allow generals to organize and arm Negroes quietly, and to proclaim emancipation in local areas. Stanton recorded, in a memo he made at the meeting, that Chase "thinks it [emancipation] a measure of great danger, and would lead to universal emancipation," unsettling the government's fiscal position.

Seward favored enlisting Negro troops but argued strenuously against emancipation. It would induce foreign nations to intervene in the war, he said, because their cotton supply would be endangered. Lincoln should announce emancipation only when the war took a turn for the better, so that it might be heralded by a victory, attended by "fife and drum and public spirit."

According to the unsupported testimony of Frank B. Carpenter, the artist, who claimed to have obtained the information from Lincoln himself, the President was so impressed by Seward's argument that he decided to withhold the proclamation until a more propitious time. Though Carpenter did not say so specifically, it has been inferred that Lincoln reached this decision before leaving the cabinet meeting. But there is evidence to indicate that Lincoln left the meeting undecided, chiefly because of Chase's opposition; that after giving the matter further thought he decided to issue the proclamation the next day; and that the delay afforded Seward an opportunity to bring a new influence to bear upon Lincoln in the person of Thurlow Weed.

Having talked to Lincoln before the cabinet meeting, Cutting saw him again that afternoon. Lincoln told him he intended to issue the proclamation the next day. But that night Weed got to Lincoln and persuaded him to change his mind, arguing that the proclamation could not be enforced and that it would be folly to make an empty gesture that would offend the border slave states.

A letter from Count Gurowski, a State Department translator, to Governor Andrew confirms Cutting's statement that the emancipation edict had been sidetracked through the interposition of Weed. Another letter, from Wolcott, who had, through Stanton, secondhand knowledge of what happened at the cabinet meeting, confirms the view that Chase, the most radical of all the cabinet members, was chiefly responsible for staying Lincoln's hand. Wolcott wrote Pamphila: "We all plied him [Chase] so vigorously, that he came round next morning, but Seward had worked so industriously, in the meantime that for the present at least,—that golden moment has passed away, and *Chase* must be held responsible for delaying or defeating the greatest act of justice, statesmanship and civilization, of the last four thousand years." Whatever Chase or Stanton felt concerning freedom for the Negro, by the second year of the war it was only a matter of timing, and in the cabinet Stanton's position was clear.

Part three

Bibliographic Essay

Because of the importance of the decision to emancipate the slaves, the subject has received special attention in the general works on the Civil War. The best examples are Allan Nevins, *The War for the Union*, 4 vols. (New York, 1959-71), J.G. Randall and David Donald, *The Civil War and Reconstruction* (Lexington, Mass., 1969), and Bruce Catton, *The Centennial History of the Civil War*, 3 vols. (New York, 1961-65). James Ford Rhodes, *The History of the United States from the Compromise of 1850 to the Final Restoration of Home Rule in the South*, 7 vols. (New York, 1891-1913), is still readable.

The biographies of Lincoln also deal with the subject in considerable detail. The best one-volume treatments are Benjamin P. Thomas, *Abraham Lincoln* (New York, 1952), and Reinhard H. Luthin, *The Real Abraham Lincoln* (Englewood Cliffs, N.J., 1960). John J. Nicolay and John Hay, *Abraham Lincoln: A History*, 10 vols. (New York, 1890), remains the most complete account, but for the war years has been superseded by J.G. Randall, *Lincoln the President*, 4 vols. (New York, 1945-55; vol. 4 completed by Richard N. Current). Carl Sandburg, *Abraham Lincoln: The War Years*, 4 vols. (New York, 1939) is the most beautifully written of the biographies.

The best general histories of the blacks in America are John Hope Franklin, *From Slavery to Freedom* (New York, 1967) and August Meier and Elliott Rudwick, *From Plantation to Ghetto* (New York, 1970). Racial prejudices are examined in George M. Frederickson, *The Black Image in the White Mind* (New York, 1971), and William R. Stanton, *The Leopard's Spots* (Chicago, 1960). Racial conditions in the Northern states are the subject of Leon Litwak, *North of Slavery* (Chicago, 1961), Eugene H. Berwanger, *The Frontier Against Slavery* (Urbana, Ill., 1967), and Jacque Voegeli, *Free But Not Equal: The Midwest and the Negro During the Civil War* (Chicago, 1967).

The standard work on the Emancipation Proclamation is John Hope Franklin, *The Emancipation Proclamation* (Garden City, N.Y., 1963). Other books on the subject include Frank Donovan, *Mr. Lincoln's Proclamation* (New York, 1964) and William O. Douglas, *Mr. Lincoln and the Negro* (New York, 1963). Charles Eberstadt, "Lincoln's Emancipation Proclamation," *The New Colophon*, 3 (1950): 312-55, details the mechanics of the writing of the document. Further particulars may be found in David M. Bates, *Lincoln in the Telegraph Office* (New York, 1907), Charles E. Hamlin, *The Life and Times of Hannibal Hamlin* (Cambridge, Mass., 1899), and Francis B. Carpenter, *Six Months at the White House with Abraham Lincoln* (New York, 1867, also published in 1868 under the title, *The Inner Life of Abraham Lincoln*). Benjamin Quarles, *Lincoln and the Negro* (New York, 1962) and *The Negro and the Civil War* (Boston, 1953) are indispensable.

Contemporary or near-contemporary accounts and reminiscences include Isaac N. Arnold, *The History of Abraham Lincoln and the Overthrow of Slavery* (Chicago, 1866), James G. Blaine, *Twenty Years of Congress*, 2 vols. (Norwich, Con., 1884); George S. Boutwell, *The Lawyer, the Statesman and the Soldier* (New York, 1887), Carl Schurz, *The Reminiscences of Carl Schurz*, 3 vols., (New York, 1907-08), and Henry Wilson, *History of the Rise and Fall of the Slave Power in America*, 3 vols. (Boston, 1876).

Lincoln's attitude towards the radicals has been the subject of controversy. T. Harry Williams, *Lincoln and the Radicals* (Madison, Wis., 1941), sees the president as a moderate harassed by radical opponents, a point of view also shared by William B. Hesseltine, *Lincoln and the War Governors* (New York, 1955), Burton J. Hendrick, *Lincoln's War Cabinet* (Boston, 1946), and the previously cited works by J.G. Randall. David Donald, *Abraham Lincoln Reconsidered* (New York, 1956), *Charles Sumner and the Rights of Man* (New York, 1970), and *Devils Facing Zionwards* in *Grant, Lee, Lincoln and the Radicals*, ed., Grady McWhiney (Evanston, Ill., 1964) minimizes the alleged conflict between the president and his antislavery critics. A similar approach may be found in Hans L. Trefousse, *The Radical Republicans* (New

York, 1969), Harold M. Hyman, ed., *The Radical Republicans and Reconstruction, 1861-1870* (Indianapolis, 1967), and Herman Belz, *Reconstructing the Union* (Ithaca, N.Y., 1969).

Unfavorable accounts of Lincoln's decision to emancipate have taken issue with most of the standard works on the subject. Ralph Korngold, *Thaddeus Stevens* (New York, 1955) portrays the president's policy as one of deliberate delay, while Lerone Bennett, Jr., "Was Abe Lincoln a White Supremacist?" *Ebony* 23 (February, 1968), answers the question substantially in the affirmative. A good summary of conflicting evidence will be found in Richard N. Current, *The Lincoln Nobody Knows* (New York, 1958).

Important biographies of members of Lincoln's cabinet include Benjamin P. Thomas and Harold M. Hyman, *Stanton* (New York, 1962), Erwin S. Bradley, *Simon Cameron* (Philadelphia, 1966), Glyndon G. Van Deusen, *William Henry Seward* (New York, 1967), John Niven, *Gideon Welles* (New York, 1973), and Marvin R. Cain, *Lincoln's Attorney General: Edward Bates of Missouri* (Columbia, Missouri, 1965).

Lincoln's skill in various fields has often been demonstrated. Robert S. Harper, *Lincoln and the Press* (New York, 1951), deals with the president's relations with the newspapers, while Jay Monaghan, *Diplomat in Carpet Slippers* (Indianapolis, 1945), emphasizes the Emancipator's success in foreign affairs.

The colonization movement has been treated in detail by P.J. Staudenraus in *The African Colonization Movement, 1816-1865* (New York, 1961). James M. McPherson, *The Struggle for Equality* (Princeton, 1964) shows that the abolitionists did not cease their agitation during the war, and Dudley Taylor Cornish, *The Sable Arm* (New York, 1966), traces the history of the black troops and their contribution. The standard work on the Sea Islands is Willie Lee Rose, *Rehearsal for Reconstruction: The Port Royal Experiment* (Indianapolis, 1964).

The best treatment of the constitutional issues of the period is Harold M. Hyman, *A More Perfect Union* (New York, 1973). It supersedes J.G. Randall, *Constitutional Problems Under Lincoln* (Urbana, Ill., 1951). The bureaucratic realities affecting any decision may be studied in A. Howard Meneeley, *The War Department, 1861* (New York, 1928), and in Leonard D. White, *The Jacksonians* (New York, 1954).

The most important sources for any research on the emancipation problem include Roy P. Basler, ed., *The Collected Works of Abraham Lincoln*, 9 vols. (New Brunswick, 1953-55), Howard K. Beale, ed., *Diary of Gideon Welles*, 3 vols. (New York, 1960), David Donald, ed., *Inside Lincoln's Cabinet: The Civil War Diaries of Salmon P. Chase* (New York, 1954), Theodore C. Pease and J.G. Randall, eds., *The Diary of Orville Hickman Browning*, 2 vols. (Springfield, Ill., 1927-33), Tyler Dennett, ed., *Lincoln and the Civil War in the Diaries and Letters of John Hay* (New York, 1939), and Noah Brooks, *Washington in Lincoln's Time*, ed. Herbert Mitgang (New York, 1958). Other sources include Frederick Bancroft, ed., *Speeches, Correspondence, and Political Papers of Carl Schurz*, 6 vols. (New York, 1913), Charles Sumner, *The Works of Charles Sumner*, 15 vols. (Boston, 1870-83), Frank Moore, ed., *The Rebellion Record*, 12 vols. (New York, 1862-68), and Edward McPherson, ed., *The Political History of the United States of America, During the Great Rebellion* (Washington, 1865). Various government publications, especially the *Congressional Globe* and *The War of the Rebellion: . . . Official Records of the Union and Confederate Armies*, 128 vols. (Washington, 1880-91), are fundamental to any study of the period.

Among the newspapers of the time, the Springfield *Republican* and the *New York Times* represent moderate Republican opinion; the New York

Tribune, the Chicago *Tribune*, the Cincinnati *Gazette*, and the St. Louis *Democrat*, the radical point of view, and the New York *World*, the Columbus *Crisis*, and the Chicago *Times*, the Democratic. Leading periodicals, such as *Harper's Weekly* and *Monthly*, and the *Atlantic Monthly* also contain valuable information.

Index